BEYOND MY DREAMS

DR. BILL MAHER
with Bob Whitmore

Beyond My Dreams

ISBN 1 889893 03 X

Published by
EMERALD HOUSE GROUP, INC.
1 Chick Springs Road, Suite 206
Greenville, South Carolina 29609

FORWARD

When I first met Bill Maher, I knew that a lifelong friendship had begun. He really never has met a stranger. He has an unusual ability to sense when people are either uncomfortable or just curious about his handicap and can immediately put them at ease. His genuine wisdom, ready smile and true humility are the fruit of a life that has been in the crucible of Christian suffering. His sense of humor is obviously a spiritual gift. He always knows the balance between just having fun and staying serious.

Those who know him already will know him better after reading this book. You will know how he is able to see beyond the outward circumstances of life and give insight on so many different situations. You will understand better his rare ability to comfort and to discern when comfort is needed. I have lost count of the times while staying in our home that I have found him just listening and offering kind words of encouragement to my wife or one of the children. Pastors listen to a lot of problems and it is all too easy to become "professional" as we listen. We need what Bro. Maher has: a genuine ability to comfort born of being comforted by the Lord Himself.

What neither he, nor most who should have encouraged him along the way realized in the early years was known to God all along. You'll laugh through tears as you read the story of a young man who is living a life beyond his dreams. As you read, you can't help wondering how many other young Billy Mahers there are around us that could be a Dr. Bill Maher someday. God is to be praised for the wonderful way He has worked in and through this man's life. Bill Maher is to be commended for the wonderful way he has served the Lord under circumstances that would have discouraged most others from the start. As you read, you will probably ask yourself the question that comes to me so often when I am with this man who is like a father to me, "If he has done this with the Lord's help, what could I do if I would really trust Him myself?"

John C. Vaughn
Greenville, South Carolina
October, 1996

This book is dedicated to my Lord and Savior, Christ Jesus, for without Him I could not have accomplished anything and there would be no story to tell. I also dedicate this to my wife, Elizabeth June Barney Maher, who has stood by me through all the years of trials and testing, and who has shared the blessings of serving our Savior. Without her help, I would not have been able to accomplish nearly so much. And last of all, to Bob Whitmore for taking time to edit the story of the laughter and heartaches we were allowed to experience in the will of God.

"But when thou makest a feast, call the poor, the maimed, the lame, the blind: And thou shalt be blessed"
Luke 14:13-14

1

A Tough Beginning

Bill Maher paced restlessly back and forth in his living room. Another low groan echoed through the house. He glanced nervously at the clock and wondered, Where is the doctor? His wife, Margaret, was having hard labor with her first child. Although Margaret was attended by a midwife, the doctor had given strict instructions that the baby should not be born until he arrived.

As he paced, Bill reflected on his good luck. This year, 1928, had been hard economically on many of his neighbors in Lorain, Ohio, but he was still working long hours as a clerk at the Cleveland Electric Illuminate Company. Although his first wife had died several years before, leaving him with two young daughters, Bill's second wife Margaret had proved to be a wonderful stepmother. And now Margaret was going to have a child to add to their family.

Bill remembered how thrilled they were when the doctor told them that Margaret was expecting. Even the girls were excited, hoping for a sister to help them with their household chores. Bill, however, wanted a boy, so he could name him William Thomas Maher. He would be the fourth generation to carry that name.

The Mahers prepared for their new addition by painting and furnishing a room for the baby. Friends and relatives gave baby showers for Margaret. The Mahers' excitement grew as the time for the birth drew nearer. Margaret went to Dr. Adair for regular check-ups, and everything seemed to be fine. Bill and Margaret had no money for a hospital stay, so they asked the doctor if the baby could be born at home. Dr. Adair had seen no problems that would prevent it, and he gave his approval. Now today, June 7, appeared to be the big day.

Margaret's labor pains started in the morning, so Bill sent for the midwife. He also sent word to Dr. Adair. The midwife arrived after a short time, and the Mahers excitedly anticipated the birth. Now it was late afternoon, and still no baby, and no Dr. Adair. Yet another moan from Margaret interrupted his thoughts. *Where is Dr. Adair?*

Finally Dr. Adair arrived. He hurried to the room where the midwife was attending Margaret. Soon the midwife emerged with a somber expression on her face. "Mr. Maher, your wife has had some complications. The baby was born at 6:45, but your wife is bleeding a lot. The doctor is trying to get it stopped."

"Is she going to be all right?" Bill asked.

"She should be, if the doctor can stop the bleeding. At 28, she's young, and strong. The doctor can tell you more." The midwife had turned to go back to assist the doctor when Bill asked, "What about the baby?"

The midwife turned slowly. "Mr. Maher, we were so busy working on your wife that I'm afraid I can't tell you much. But I think the baby is dead. It didn't cry when it was born, and I just put it in the crib." Bill was stunned. "And by the way, it was a boy."

Bill sank into a chair, his head in his hands. He had already lost a wife, and now he had lost a son, and may yet lose Margaret.

Long minutes passed before Dr. Adair came from Margaret's room. "Bill, as you know there were unexpected complications regarding the birth. Margaret lost a lot of blood, but her condition is stable now and she should recover with some rest. The baby is alive, but I'm afraid he is severely afflicted. We will have to run tests to know how bad it is or if he will live long."

Dr. Adair left, and Bill went in to see Margaret. She was weak, but she attempted a smile. She was cradling the baby in her arms. Bill noticed that the left side of the baby's head was flat and misshapen.

"Bill," Margaret whispered, "I want you to meet William Thomas Maher." Bill just stared at the fragile creature in Margaret's arms. "Bill, I think he will live. I think he's a fighter to have survived his birth. Let's call him Billy."

Soon Bill and Margaret found themselves sitting in Dr. Adair's office. They had brought little Billy in for tests to determine the extent of his affliction. Dr. Adair looked over a sheaf of papers, and then said, "It appears your child has severe cerebral palsy. It is unlikely that he will ever be able to learn or do anything to take care of himself. He may be like a vegetable. Why don't we just put him away in a mental institution and forget he was born? After all, you can have other children, and you won't have to bother with caring for an afflicted child."

"Put him away and treat him like an animal after all the trouble I went through having him?" Margaret cried in shocked horror. "Absolutely not! We love our son, and we'll find a doctor somewhere to help us." So Bill and Margaret made the fateful decision to raise a severely handicapped child during the worst years of the Great Depression. Their lives would never be the same, and certainly would never be considered "normal" by others. Yet I am glad for their decision, for I was the handicapped baby they called Billy.

LIFE WITH THE HANDICAPPED

"Now girls, Billy will not be able to do what other brothers can do," Mom told my older sisters, Lenore and Dorothy.

"Why?" they wanted to know.

"Well, Billy is different from other babies. He is handicapped." Lenore and Dorothy didn't understand then what that meant. They just knew that I got a lot more attention than they did. My grandparents Stale, on my mother's side, came to help. They baby-sat so my mother could rest, took me to the doctor, and did hundreds of other things to relieve my parents' burden. My mother's brother, Uncle George, also helped, as did an aunt and uncle on my dad's side.

My parents had decided that I should be treated as though I were normal, and all of my relatives tried to abide by their wishes. Sometimes, though, this was hard to do when nothing about me was normal. My neck was too weak to hold up my head, so my head was propped up by pillows. My arms and legs were stiff and drawn up close to my body. The doctors said that my limbs should be pulled away from my body and straightened so that my joints would not lock into position. Of course, this was very painful for my contracted muscles, and I would cry as I got my daily physical therapy. My tongue was rolled so tightly in my mouth that it was hard for me to swallow, or even smile. Saliva ran down my face, causing a rash around my mouth and chin, so those caring for me had to apply cold cream to ease the pain of the rash.

When I was two years old I contracted mumps and measles at the same time. The illnesses combined to leave me even weaker and added yet another handicap to my list of afflictions. My parents soon realized that I was not paying attention to them anymore when they talked to me. They knew something was wrong and rushed me to a doctor.

The doctor gravely examined my afflicted body. "I hate to tell you the sad news," he said to my parents. "I seems you have had nothing but bad news concerning your son. His eardrums have ruptured, and he will never be able to hear again." My parents left the doctor's office with tears coursing down their faces. Their child's arms, legs, and tongue could not function as they should, and now this!

Mom and Dad headed back home. It was time to let the rest of their family know about the added affliction. They explained to my sisters that I was now deaf. "But how is Billy going to learn what he needs to know?" they asked. My parents had no answer.

By this time many doctors in the area knew about the Mahers' afflicted son. When researchers developing therapies for those afflicted with cerebral palsy looked for people to take part in their experiments, our local doctors sent them to us. They would ask my parents for permission to work on my body along with others who had afflictions. My parents thought they had nothing to lose, and perhaps I would benefit from some of the experimental treatments. So as a small child I joined a group of the afflicted who became human guinea pigs. These researchers tried all sorts of treatments. Even chiropractors got into the the act. About all I remember about the therapy is the pain. "No pain, no gain" could have been their motto! "Nothing good will come out of it unless there is pain," they told my parents. If a treatment worked, they would continue it; if not, they would stop and try to figure out why it didn't work and devise a new treatment. Receiving these treatments sometimes meant that I would have to stay in a hospital for a week, a month, or even longer. When I came back home, my mother would continue any treatments they told her to do.

Taking care of me must have been a tremendous hardship on my family. Day after day my mom and dad would pull my arms and legs away from my body. Stretching these muscles turned my limbs black and blue with bruises. When they would let go, my arms would snap back so hard that soon my chest was bruised as well. The pain would cause me to cry, and often my mom would cry along with me. But Mom never let my crying cause her to stop the exercises, for she saw that they were working. My limbs began to move more freely. Sometimes she would make up songs or poems that went with various exercises. Although my deafness kept me from hearing her words, I understood that my mother loved me. The exercises were just as painful, but it helped that she tried to bear the pain with me. Even Lenore and Dorothy would join in the fun helping with Billy's exercises as they sang Mother's songs. "You girls are a big help to your brother," she told them. "Thank you for helping. If we all keep helping Billy, one day he will be able to do all the things that you girls are able to do." She had no way of knowing this for sure, but she kept a positive outlook.

"What about Billy's tongue?" Mom asked the therapist. My tongue was still rolled up tight inside my mouth. The therapist grabbed a tissue, reached inside my mouth, and pulled out my tongue. Ouch! I bit down hard on his hand, and it was his turn to feel some pain! But somehow it had to be done if I would ever have the use of my tongue. Now my mom thought up a strategy.

Without the use of my arms, I was still totally dependent on my mother or sisters to feed me. Was I really going to bite the hands that fed me? I soon understood that if I wanted to be fed, I first had to allow my mom or dad to pull out my tongue. I have to admit now that I'm glad they were willing to inflict pain on me for my long-term good, but I wasn't glad about it then.

Because many of my treatments were experimental, most of them were unsuccessful. A few were even funny. Once I was given 179 shots of special medication to relax my muscles and allow them to move more freely. It didn't work, but it prompted my dad to tell me, "Don't drink anything, Billy. I'm afraid you'll spring a leak!" Another time, heat treatments were tried for several months, but they didn't seem to help. Still another time they tried freezing me. That didn't work either, and I was glad because I was cold.

How many times I wanted to give up, but not Mom and Dad. They just would not accept my affliction. "He is going to do what others can do," they would tell others. "It will just take him longer, that's all."

Physical therapy exercises, working along with a chiropractor, seemed to help the most. Daily I went through a regular exercise routine, which included stretching my tongue. By the time I was five years old I could walk after a fashion by dragging my feet. I still couldn't lift my feet like I should. I communicated through grunts and hand signs, for I had not yet learned to talk.

FIRST CONTACT WITH CHRISTIANS

Although our relatives were sympathetic and understanding of my afflictions, some of our friends and neighbors were not. As I grew older, my parents tried to give me as normal a childhood as possible. This meant I played outdoors around other children. Their parents could not believe that my mother and father really wanted me. To them I was like an animal that no parents would want, but common decency obligated my family to care for me. Because their parents talked about me and made fun of me at home, some children were mean to me. Although I could not hear, I had learned to read lips, and I was deeply hurt by their taunts.

Sometimes, if my sisters were not present, the other children would kick me and spit on me and call me names. Teenagers were the worst. Yet some of them faithfully attended all services at their churches. A few even had the nerve to ask me to become a Christian! If what they had was Christianity, I wanted no part of it. Their parents would ask my father, "What great sin did you commit that your son was born like this?" He was so hurt by their insensitive remarks that he became bitter at those who called themselves Christians.

Apparently these people had never read Leviticus 19:14: "Thou shalt not curse the deaf, nor put a stumblingblock before the blind, but shalt fear thy God: I am the Lord." In other words, Christians should realize that God made the afflicted the way they are for a purpose and no one should take advantage of them because of their afflictions.

One day after I returned from physical therapy at the hospital, I decided to practice my walking in front of our house. Rain had fallen earlier that day, but now the sun was coming out. I was excited about walking, because I could tell I was getting better. Maybe I would even be able to run and play baseball if I kept working. As I labored down the sidewalk dragging my feet and swinging my arms, a lady known as a Christian walked toward me from the opposite direction. Because I couldn't get out of her way fast enough, she pushed me down into the mud and walked past me. I wasn't hurt physically, but I was so shocked I cried out loud. Mother came dashing from the house to see what was wrong. I was covered with mud, and I made signs with my hands to tell Mother what had happened. The lady had stopped, and my mother asked her if what I said was true. "Yes," she haughtily admitted. "He doesn't belong where civilized people walk. He should be taken out to the woods where all the other animals are." Then she spun on her heel and walked away with her nose in the air.

Mother led me indoors. I was crying my heart out. I couldn't understand why people wanted to hurt me. I made signs to tell Mother that I wasn't going to walk outside again.

"Yes you are, Billy. You have as much right to the sidewalk as anyone else." She took me back outside. "Billy, don't let anyone stop you. You can do it, and you will do it. Giving up is not in our vocabulary."

These incidents were extremely painful to our family. My parents wanted nothing to do with Christianity, and neither did I.

2

A NEW NEIGHBORHOOD

Soon my family moved to a new neighborhood. We rented a two-story house right across the street from Lake Erie. In the winter the cold north wind blew old Jack Frost across the lake to paint our windows. I used to watch him work as I fell asleep. Our front room was so cold that we used it to store food during the winter months. Who needed a freezer? We had one from December to April.

The kitchen was the central gathering place. A potbellied stove radiated warmth, and the room was often filled with the wonderful smells of homemade bread and baked goodies. There our family gathered for conversation, and company often ended up in the kitchen. Even the dog was allowed in when it was too cold for him outside.

I was attending kindergarten at this time. I enjoyed it because children at that age all have trouble doing things and they did not seem to notice that anything was wrong with me. I was still receiving daily physical therapy, which caused me to miss a lot of kindergarten.

When March arrived, Dad got an idea. "Let's have a garden," he said. We put on our coats, as it was still cold, and he took me out in the yard and showed me where "we" would have a garden. "There's a shovel in the shed," he said. I shuffled over to the shed and returned with the shovel. I handed it to him, but he told me I was going to do the digging. What had happened to the "us"? Dad said it was good therapy for me, but to me it seemed like plain old work. I dragged my feet over to where I was going to dig. I had to pick up my foot to place it on the shovel, then wrap my arms around the handle because I couldn't grasp it with my hands.

When I finished digging, I had a stiff back, sore muscles, and raw blisters. Then I got to hoe, rake, and plant seeds. Dad did not accept my afflictions as an excuse not to work. As far as he was concerned, I could work like any other boy my age. At this point I didn't know if I liked being treated as though I were "normal" if it meant working like this. I soon learned that my parents would make hard work a part of my life.

Springtime meant spring cleaning. My sisters helped my mom clean the house, but guess who beat the rugs and swabbed the porch? I wrapped my arms around the mop handle and swabbed away. The rug beater had a handle with big wire loops coming out of it. I would grab it awkwardly and smack the rugs as hard as I could. Often I would lose my grip and the beater would fly out of my hands.

My mom and sisters washed the inside of the windows while I washed the outside. Holding the rags to wash the windows or dust furniture was no problem. Once the rag was in my right hand, my stiff fingers could not let go of it. To turn the rag I had to grab it with my left hand, pull it from my right hand, and jam it back in my stiff fingers. It was slow, but I got the job done. At first Dad washed the second-story windows, but when I got older I got that job too.

Of course, I thought I did all the work. Lenore and Dorothy did their share, but I wanted them to do mine as well. I played on Mom's sympathy to get them to help me. "Mom," I whined, "you know my hands and feet don't work right. Tell them to help me." She would do it, which at times made me very unpopular with my sisters. I loved to tease them, but it didn't take Mom long to figure out what I was doing. "Mom, he's doing it again," they would cry, and I would get a spanking.

In the winter time I shoveled snow, which was abundant at our house. My sisters would gang up on me in any snowball fights. I think they were trying to get even with me for the dirty tricks I played on them!

Saturday was a work day at the Maher house no matter what the season. We cleaned the house from top to bottom. Again, my sisters and I did most of the work. Mom would say, "When you're done with your work, you can go out to play." Dot, Lenore, and I took turns doing chores as fast as we could. One would use the non-electric sweeper to clean the carpets, while someone else made beds or dusted. Our furniture had fancy carved grooves that made dusting difficult. Before we could go out to play, we had to pass Mom's inspection. She would rub her fingers over the furniture. If it was still dusty, we had to do it over. All the rooms we cleaned were checked and double-checked by that tough inspector we called Mom. By the time we passed inspection we were often too tired to go out and play. By teaching us to work, my parents kept us out of trouble.

Summer was my favorite season. I loved to go swimming in Lake Erie, and the doctors encouraged my swimming because it was good therapy. Finally, some physical therapy that was painless and fun. My mother and sisters took me across the street to the swimming beach as often as they could. I began to enjoy fishing, and when I wasn't swimming I would try my luck at catching the big one. Dad would join us when he didn't have to work. Swimming and fishing, however, came only after my chores—working in the garden, cutting the grass, taking care of the flowers, and whatever else needed to be done around the yard.

When the neighbors would see me out working, they would say to my parents, "Poor Billy. Why do you make him work so hard? Don't you know he is handicapped?" At that time I would put on my most pitiful expression. I didn't care how I got out of work, just so long as I didn't have to do it. My parents, however, weren't fooled by my act. "Mind your own business," my parents would reply to the neighbors. "In this family, everybody works." The neighbors didn't really think I was overworked; they just thought because I was afflicted I wasn't supposed to know what I was doing.

By the time I was six, I was walking well. I couldn't run very well, though, so when I played tag with my sisters I was "it" most of the time. When I got tired of being "it," I would squeal to Mom. "Girls, it's not nice to take advantage of Billy's handicap. Stop teasing him. You take turns being 'it' for a while." That spoiled the girls' fun, so we'd all troop into the house. We would sit on the sofa and stick out our tongues and make faces at each other until we started to giggle. Then we would play some more.

We also liked to play hide-and-seek. Since I couldn't hear, they could laugh and talk while they were hiding. When it was my turn to hide, they had no trouble finding me because I made all kinds of noise I didn't know I was making.

GOING TO SCHOOL

In September 1934 it was time for me to enter public school. All kids went to school, so my parents thought I should too. I was excited as I assembled the papers, pencils, and books necessary for me to be a first-grader at Irving School on the west side of Lorain. I would have to walk to school no matter what the weather was like, for there were no school buses back then. Besides, my parents said walking would be good for me. There was just one problem with school: I couldn't hear, talk, or use my hands.

My mother told the teacher, "Billy must be able to hear something. If he looks at me when I talk, he always knows what I'm saying. When he looks away, just like all kids, he doesn't pay attention. So just make him look at you." What they didn't know was that I had learned to read lips. Because I did it, I thought everyone could do it. Apparently my teacher and parents had never heard of lip-reading.

Somehow I learned to read by watching the teacher's lips. But writing seemed impossible. When I tried to write with a pencil, I gripped the pencil so tightly that it broke in two, or I pressed down so hard that the point broke. Most of our writing was done with fountain pens, but they fared little better in my hands. In addition, they had to be dipped into an ink bottle. By the end of the day I would be covered with ink. My mom had to scrub my clothes with a big bar of yellow cleaning soap, but even that failed to remove the stains completely.

My excitement about school was wearing off fast. This seemed to be just another name for work. Not only did I have to learn English, math, history, geography, spelling, and writing in class, but I had homework too. Every night Mom and Dad made sure I did my homework right. If I didn't I had to do it over, no matter how long it took. They seemed to have no pity at all for the afflicted.

These years weren't all work, though. I especially enjoyed visiting my grandparents. My sisters didn't often go, but I didn't understand why. They preferred to go to their mother's parents who lived in Cleveland. They knew all their aunts and uncles and cousins on their mother's side of the family. It took me a long time to figure out that we had different mothers and therefore different sets of relatives.

I spent a lot of time during the summers at my mother's parents house. I enjoyed being spoiled by them. They had a beautiful, two-story brick house with an attic and a full basement. On the second floor was a screened porch. I liked to sleep out there when the weather was nice. The basement contained a coal furnace and a wine cellar. I learned to roller skate down there on the cement floor. Of course, it was harder for me than for most other kids. I took lots of spills, and my knees and elbows suffered accordingly. My mother got upset with her parents for allowing me to skate, but they told her, "If he is going to be a normal child, then he is going to learn to take his bumps like anyone else. You can't always be around to protect him. You have to let him learn like all other children." Mom kept quiet, and I got more bumps.

As the conductor on the old Nickel Plate train, Grandpa got a lot of free passes to ride from Lorain to Bellview. He often took me along on train rides. He let me follow him down the aisles as he took up tickets. It was also fun eating in the dining car.

My grandpa had several hobbies he practiced down in the cellar, one of which was making wine from grapes or dandelions. One time I was down there skating when he noticed I was falling down more than usual, but I didn't seem to get hurt, and each time I fell, I laughed as if it were some big joke. He found out I had been nipping at his stock of wine. I got the whipping of my life! When I got home and my parents found out, I got another whipping. It was a couple of days before I could sit down comfortably. But I never again touched Grandpa's wine.

There was a dolly to haul things back and forth between the basement and the kitchen. I loved to ride in that thing. If Mom was there, I wasn't allowed to ride in it, but left alone with

Grandma I had fun. Parents spoil fun, but grandparents spoil kids.

Sometimes grandparents could be like parents. Grandma had a clothes chute from the second floor to the basement. I often dropped a ball down the chute, but once I dropped a frog down there instead. I couldn't hear my grandma scream, but the neighbors could. "Billy, you'll be the death of me if you keep it up," my grandma scolded. Then I got a spanking.

My grandparents would take me to one of my favorite places, the ice cream parlor. I was forced to straighten my tongue to lick the ice cream cones. This was the best kind of physical therapy I could imagine.

Uncle George, Mom's brother, and my dad decided to teach me to play baseball. Dad had played in the minor league in Seattle, Washington, before he was married. Uncle George was a catcher for a local team, and he somehow thought I could be a pitcher when I got older. Now how was this going to work? I had all I could do to walk, let alone run bases. I could hardly write, so how was I going to catch and throw a ball? Yet they made up their minds they would teach me to play ball. They tried to teach me all they knew about fielding the ball, throwing, and catching. Even my grandpa got involved. But there was one who had more confidence than any of them that I could be a ball player—my great-grandmother; she would throw the ball to me, and I would try to catch it. If it fell to the ground, I had to scoop it up like a real ball player. She was amazing.

My Uncle Ernie, my dad's brother, worked for the electric company. After storms he would repair high voltage wires, which made him a very brave fellow in my estimation. He too joined in teaching me baseball, with Aunt Fannie, his wife, taking part as cheerleader. They lived only a short distance from us, and I spent many hours at their house.

LEARNING TO MAKE MONEY

One summer afternoon Grandpa gave me a job. "I'll give you twenty-five cents if you mow the grass," he said. I thought that was a good deal. During the Great Depression years, money was scarce. But how could I get the money without having to do the work? I knew a boy who would do just about anything for money, so I went to his house and offered him the job for five pennies. He mowed the grass, and I told him to come back after Grandpa came home from work and I would pay him.

When Grandpa came home from his job at the railroad, he saw the yard was mowed. I asked him to pay me with two dimes and five pennies. "Why do you want it that way?" he asked.

"I have a special reason, Grandpa."

He went along with my request to see what I was up to. Soon the boy showed up, and I gave him the five pennies we had agreed on. He went away happy, and so did I.

My grandpa thought it was funny. He was actually proud of me. When my parents came to get me, he said to them, "You'll have nothing to worry about. Billy has a good head on his shoulders." Then he proceeded to tell them what I did.

My mother wasn't proud of me at all; she was furious! "The boy should have gotten all the money, Billy. He did all the work," she scolded. "Billy is getting lazy," she said to my dad.

"Wait a minute," Grandpa interrupted. "It took brains to figure out this scheme. Billy can make a living using his brain. He can have others working for him. What's wrong with that? I work for a railroad company that is owned by someone else."

Mom began to calm down. Dad smiled and said, "Maybe someday Billy will take care of himself and us."

SPECIAL EDUCATION

I didn't feel very smart at the end of fifth grade, however. I failed to make passing marks. What a horrible feeling. My mom and dad were very upset and protested to the teacher and the principal. "We are sorry," the principal said, "but Billy cannot keep up with the other students. He has so much trouble writing that we cannot read it. We have no idea if he can spell or add. It would be better for him to repeat the fifth grade. Or maybe you should check into the special school in Elyria. It's for the deaf and hard-of-hearing, and it may meet his needs better than we can. I think Billy would be comfortable there."

My parents took the principal's advice. We went over to Franklin School in Elyria. It was something like a one-room school, with its one room full of deaf and hard-of-hearing students of all ages and grades. My parents were impressed by the teacher, Mrs. Mary Spoerl. In addition to studying the regular academic subjects, the students were also taught lip-reading. Although I had already learned to read lips to some extent, there was plenty of room for improvement. Students would pass on to higher grade levels according to the work they had completed regardless of the time it took. Right after Labor Day I began going to Franklin School. I had to rise before dawn to be ready for the 30-mile trip to school in our 1936 Chevrolet.

Mrs. Spoerl employed techniques that helped me with my writing. She had me write my name and various numbers on the blackboard. I had such poor control of my movements that my name would take up the whole blackboard. My stiff arms, wrists, and fingers shook badly. But she didn't let me quit, and my writing began to improve.

Lip-reading was not as easy as a hearing person might think. Mrs. Spoerl would show an object, then form the words with her lips. Next, she would take a simple story book and read it very slowly while we watched her lips. Then we had to tell her what she had read. If we were wrong, she would read the story over again. When we understood what she read, she would go to another book and read faster. We went through this process until we could understand her when she read at the pace of normal conversation. Then she read books with harder vocabulary.

Another drill helped us learn to talk. Mrs. Spoerl put our names on the blackboard and formed each name with her lips while you did the same. Then we students would slowly read aloud a simple book to one another. This helped us learn to speak as well as improve our lip-reading ability, which would enable us to carry on a conversation with a hearing person.

Most hearing people do not realize how hard it is for a deaf person to learn to talk. Because he cannot hear others, he doesn't know how words are supposed to sound. And he can't hear himself either. So a deaf person's speech may be abnormal, hitting high and low notes that sound strange to a hearing person. The deaf have to learn to keep their voices on an even keel, which is very hard. And all the time we were learning these basic skills that "normal" people take for granted, we were also studying regular academic subjects.

Franklin School was right next to Elyria High School, and they allowed us to use their facilities for some of our activities. The "normal" kids didn't want us playing with them, so we had our own deaf football games and other sports.

MOVING TO AVON LAKE

In the summer of 1939 my family moved to Avon Lake, Ohio, which was closer to Dad's job. My parents bought a two-story house for $4,000. The house was on a large lot with a garage and shed. It was right across the street from a farm. I was excited to have my own bedroom right across from the bathroom. There was also an open porch where I sometimes slept during the summers. I would fall asleep counting the stars.

The neighborhood was a quiet one where everyone seemed to know everyone else. As a newcomer, and handicapped besides, I was not always well-treated. It was the same old thing. Kids would spit at me or beat on me and run away laughing. I would get so mad I wanted to kill them, but I was too restricted in my movements to catch and hit them. One boy my age who would imitate the way I walked and talked earned my special hatred. One day, in my fury, I threw a hatchet at him. I missed, but not on purpose. I had intended to kill him.

During these years our family took various vacations. We saw Washington, D. C., Niagara Falls, and different attractions in Kentucky and West Virginia. There were no motels back then, so we stayed in hotels or guest homes where one could get a room along with the evening meal and breakfast, all for one price. It would take us a couple of days to go from Avon Lake to West Virginia traveling on the narrow two-lane roads. Mom would pack a picnic basket full of food and a jug of lemonade. The luggage was stowed on the running board of the car. My sisters and I would crowd into the back seat and hope that it would not rain, for then the luggage would be moved into our seat and crowd us even more.

3

FULLY INCLINED TO MISCHIEF

Some people have the mistaken idea that the afflicted are too dumb to get into mischief. When I was a boy, I was living proof that they can. When my twelfth birthday approached, I wanted a bike like the other kids had. My parents told me that they couldn't afford to get me one for my birthday, but Mom did say that I could have a birthday party. She agreed to let me invite as many kids as I could get to come. She thought it was worth the sacrifice to let me have a special birthday before I became a teenager, but she didn't know how special it was going to be.

I asked dozens of kids to come to my party. When they said they would like to come, I told them they would have to bring fifty cents if they wanted cake and ice cream. This was in addition to their birthday presents.

Finally the great day, June 7, 1940, arrived. I stood outside the door to greet each guest and pocket their money so Mom wouldn't find out. When Dad got home from work the party got underway. Everyone was enjoying the festivities. I opened my gifts, my guests sang "Happy Birthday," and we all had cake and ice cream. Then one boy asked for more. Mom told him there wasn't any more. "What do you mean?" he cried. "We paid for all the ice cream and cake we could eat!"

That liar, that's not what I said, I thought. But Mom didn't care. She was mad at me. "Billy, I can't believe what you have done. You give everyone's money back right now. I ought to make you give their presents back too."

Then Dad entered in, and was I ever glad. He often took a different view of my shenanigans. "Wait a minute," he said to Mom. He looked sternly at me. "Billy, why did you charge your guests to come to your party?" he demanded.

"Everyone else has a bike, and you said you could not afford

25

to buy me one. So I thought if I got enough money I could buy a bike," I replied. Dad's eye began to twinkle. "How much did you get?" he asked. After counting my bulging pocketful of coins, we discovered I had enough for a brand new bike. Dad thought the whole thing was funny. He was proud of me, and Mom was mad at both of us. "Billy just has a business mind," Dad said as he tried to calm Mom, "just like his grandfather said. He will be able to take care of himself," he boasted.

When I got my new bike I saw another opportunity to make a deal. I was the only kid on the block with a new bike, and I noticed that all my friends were jealous. "Hey, want to ride my new bike?" I would ask. Of course, they all did. "I'll let you ride it around the block for a quarter," I said. Soon money again filled my pocket. And these kids picked on me because they thought I was dumb!

Mom was distraught. "What will the neighbors think?" she said to Dad.

"Who cares?" Dad told her. "Billy has been picked on so much, I think it's good he's showing them he isn't stupid." Again, Dad was proud of me. With all the use my bike got, it soon looked at old as everyone else's, and business slacked off. But it was fun while it lasted.

MEETING THE SAVIOR

The Stigers were one family that was kind to me. They invited me to their church, the Avon Baptist Church. Their son, Ralph, took me to Sunday school. I saw there many of the kids who picked on me. Then we went into the church auditorium for the morning service, and there sat the woman who had pushed me in the mud and told my mom that I shouldn't be around civilized people. I don't know if she recognized me. If she noticed me, she pretended I wasn't there.

Strange as it may seem, despite the people I encountered, I enjoyed the service. I went back that evening. The pastor, Rev. V. D. Geren, preached from John 3:3: "Verily, verily, I say unto thee, except a man be born again, he cannot see the kingdom of

God." I thought he was talking about physical blindness. Because I could not use my hands well, talk well or hear, I had a great fear of getting another affliction. I did not want to go blind and not be able to see God's kingdom! My family did not go to church or read the Bible, so I was ignorant about what the Bible said.

After the service, I wanted to talk to Rev. Geren, but I needed someone who could understand me and be able to tell Rev. Geren what I was saying. Chuck Webb, a friend who was my age, acted as my interpreter.

"Pastor, I do not want to go blind!" I said.

"You are already blind," answered the pastor. What? "You're blind to the things of God," he explained. Then he began to tell me how wicked I was.

"Wait a minute," I told him. "I'm not as bad as you say. I can't hear dirty stories. I can't say bad words. I can only walk a little, and I haven't been to bad places." I felt pretty smug.

"How did you know there is such a thing as bad words and dirty stories?" he asked. I didn't have an answer. I didn't know how I knew these things. "Did you ever think bad words, or think about dirty stories? That's just as bad as saying them out loud." If that was true, I was in trouble!

Rev. Geren explained that the devil was teaching me all of these wicked things. According to John 8:44, he said, the devil was my father! Because of this, I needed God as my Father if I wanted to go to heaven. "Whoever your father is when you die, that's who you will spend eternity with." I needed to be born again into God's family. "Unless you are born again, you will go to hell with Satan. If you become God's child, you'll go to heaven to be with your Heavenly Father."

That sounded simple enough, but the devil provided me with one more alibi. "If God loves me, he ought to let me into heaven because I'm afflicted." How could God send a handicapped boy like me to hell?

Rev. Geren opened his Bible to Romans 2:11 and explained that God doesn't look at the body, but at the heart. If a person's heart is not washed in the blood of Christ, handicapped or not, that person is on the way to hell.

That night in August of 1940, two wonderful things happened. The first was I asked Christ to save me. If I had to do something to be saved, it would have been impossible, for I could hardly use my hands. If there would have been something I had to say, it would have been impossible, for I couldn't talk. But I did have faith in my heart in the finished work of Christ. Although no one else understood my prayer, God did. The second thing that happened was the result of the first. When I had walked into church that night, I had seen people I hated. When I left, I couldn't hate them anymore. II Corinthians 5:17, "Therefore if any man be in Christ, he is a new creature: old things are passed away; behold, all things are become new," was true of me. In an instant God changed my heart.

There was one boy in my neighborhood who seemed not to notice my afflictions. He just played with me as though I had no limitations. He was a Catholic boy named Bob McNally. Once not long after I was saved, we were sitting on the back steps of my house talking about what were were going to be when we grew up. Bob said he was going to be a Catholic priest. Not to be outdone, I said I would be a Baptist preacher like Rev. Geren.

HIGH SCHOOL

I continued to attend church and make progress in school. Then everything changed. On December 7, 1941, the Japanese bombed Pearl Harbor. The next day we declared war on Japan. It was all very confusing to us who could not hear the news on the radio. When we learned that men would have to go and fight the enemy, we wanted to go too. But we were too young. Besides, we could not hear and would not have a chance against the enemy. The best thing for us, we were told, was to continue with school so we could get a job at the defense plants to build weapons for our soldiers.

But we now had a problem. Gasoline was rationed, and we could no longer make the daily trip to school. Regular school was out of the question. My parents didn't know what to do. They talked to Mrs. Spoerl, and she suggested I stay with a family in

Elyria. She even found a family, the Charlestons, that I could stay with. It worked out great, for they lived only a short distance from school. Besides, they had a deaf son. His name was Weston, and we became fast friends. I would spend the week with the Charlestons, and come home on the weekends. Sometimes Weston came home with us to spend the weekend. My parents would share food rations with Weston's family, but not the gas rations. They needed them to have enough gas to make the trip to Elyria twice every weekend.

By the time I was fourteen years old, I could use my hands except for the hook finger on my left hand. I could walk almost normally. What a miracle for a boy who was never supposed to be able to do anything for himself. God was certainly at work in my life.

After five years at Franklin School, I was in the tenth grade. I had kept up academically. Over the years I had learned to move my wrists and fingers so I could write legibly. I could read lips well, and I could talk. At the end of tenth grade, we were told it was time for us to face the real world without the comfort and safety of Franklin School and Mrs. Spoerl. It was frightening to let go of this haven in a world of meanness. I moved back to my parents' house in June 1945. By this time my sisters had already finished high school. Now it was my turn to go to Avon Lake High School. I wasn't a complete stranger, for I knew some of the kids. I had played with them or gone to church with them over the years.

The people I had problems with were the teachers. The teachers and principal had no idea how much progress I had made at Franklin School. They said I should stay home, for I was not capable of learning anything. They couldn't understand that I had overcome most of my afflictions. Furthermore, I had already studied most of the hard subjects-English, algebra, geometry, history-at Elyria High School. *I'll show them,* I thought. I'll take all the hardest subjects offered in this school. Paul said in Philippians 4:13, "I can do all things through Christ." *So can I,* I thought.

On my sixteenth birthday my dad pulled a surprise on me.

"Come on, Bill. Let's go for a ride in the car."

"Where are we going?" I asked, but he just smiled. I figured he was going to take me someplace special or buy me a birthday gift. We went out on a dirt road, and Dad stopped the car. "Get out and come around on my side." I only saw him say "Get out," and I wondered what I had done to make him mad at me. Then he said again, "Get out and come around on my side of the car." This time he added, "You're going to learn how to drive." I understood this time, and he wouldn't have to repeat it a third time. I was around that car in a flash. I did indeed learn to drive.

Six months later I took my driving test. The examiner asked me two questions: "What do you do when you see a fire truck with its lights flashing?" and "What do you do when you meet an ambulance?" I answered both questions the same way: "Pull off the road and let it by."

"You know all the answers," he said. "I don't need to ask you any more questions. Let's see how well you can drive." We went out to the car. "Go around the block and park." I did that with no problem. "You are really a good driver," he said. We went back inside and I was issued a license. I was glad he hadn't asked me to back up, for I hadn't learned that yet. Still, I was one proud boy. Maybe I couldn't hear and my speech was still hard to understand, but I had a driver's license! Mom and Dad were proud too. "Now we know he can do anything anyone else can do," they bragged. Being able to drive didn't help me get to school. Although I still had to walk or ride the bus, I could show everyone that I had a license to drive.

I worked a couple of different jobs during my teen years. One was mowing a large yard for a doctor. His wife was very kind-hearted. She often worried that I was working too hard and would tell me to slow down. She would come out to get me to take a rest break and bring me lemonade or water. I enjoyed the way she spoiled me.

The other job I had was at a florist shop in Avon Lake. The owners were great people to work for. Working in their greenhouse, I learned much about raising flowers. We would sterilize the soil before planting flower seeds. After they grew and began to bloom, we took them out of that bed and planted them in another part of the greenhouse. In the summer months we planted flowers outside. We worked to have plenty of flowers available for special days such as Mother's Day, Easter, and Valentine's Day.

My employers were very patient with me. Right after I got my driver's license, they had me drive a truck loaded with dirt. Everything was fine so long as I was going forward. Then one day the boss decided to have me back the truck through a wide door at the end of the greenhouse. I was trying my best to back in when broken glass began falling all around me. I had hit the side of the greenhouse. I turned around in horror in time to see my boss yell, "Don't get out of the truck until all the glass falls." I could see he was angry. Finally I saw him say, "Now get out." I thought he was firing me, so I peddled my bike home feeling miserable.

"Why are you home now?" Mom asked. I was embarrassed to tell her what I had done, but I did. She didn't say anything, and neither did Dad when she told him what happened.

Soon I saw Mom answer the telephone. I could see her nodding her head "yes" every so often. After she hung up the phone, she told me I was to go back to work.

"Why? He fired me."

"All I know is that he said for you to get back there," Mom said.

So back I went, but I admit I didn't peddle very fast. When I arrived an unsmiling boss was waiting for me. "Why did you skip out on me?"

"You told me to get out and I did. I figured I was fired," I replied.

"Well, maybe you should be. Bill, you are a good worker, but you are a lousy driver. You will not drive the truck except to go forward. I'll teach you to back up. Is that a deal?" I said he had a deal. "Now help me pick up all of this glass," he said. He allowed me to continue working for him, and true to his word he taught me how to back up his truck.

As I grew older my hearing gradually began to return. I would never be able to hear normally, but by the time I became an adult I would be able to hear with the help of a hearing aid.

Meanwhile, I was doing passing work in high school. I even tried to get involved in extracurricular activities. One time I had a small part in a play. It was a comedy, and four of us were supposed to sing in a sad part. It was sad all right. Apparently none of us could sing, and I'm sure I was the worst. It must have been okay because the audience sure laughed.

Along with school work, I took woodworking, drama, and even cooking. All the boys had to take cooking, while the girls were made to take shop classes. We boys made believe we didn't like cooking, but we were actually proud of our prowess in the kitchen. Because we had to eat whatever we cooked or baked, we made sure we followed the recipes.

Another thing I wanted to do was be involved in sports. Everyone had to take gym class, but I wanted to play on the school football team. I enjoyed playing although I wasn't very good. I even found an outlet for my mischievous nature.

I was on the reserve team, and we always practiced against the first team. Of course, we would lose every scrimmage. I got tired of that and came up with a strategy to beat them. I called our team together and told them my plan. Since both squads used the same plays, I told them I would use my lip-reading ability to read their quarterback's lips. It would be easy from my position at right defensive end. If we knew what play they were going to run, we could stop them.

I gave my team signals to let them know if it was a run or a pass, and whether they were going to the right or to the left. We started doing great. We tackled the ball carrier before he could get anywhere. We stopped all of their passes. The coach was beside himself. He was getting madder and madder at the first team. He knew we were not that good.

After two hours, the coach called an end to practice. He was still confused and fighting mad. Before he could chew out the first team, I knew I had to confess to him what we had been doing. When he realized I was the source of the problem, he chased me all the way to the shower room. I had no idea what he was shouting, but by the look on his face it wasn't pleasant. And I knew I had better outrun him to the showers, and I did. I didn't know I could run so fast.

The coach was also my biology teacher. The next day in class he wasn't mad at me anymore. For weeks after that he would say, "Read my lips, Maher!" and laugh. He really encouraged me in many ways because he was able to see past my physical afflictions and realize that I capable of learning.

GRADUATION AND WORK

At last I completed my high school course work. It was time for graduation, and I was excited. At the ceremony, I could see my parents sitting in the audience with other parents. They beamed with pride and happiness. The speeches were made, and finally it was time for us to receive our diplomas. The graduates' names were called in alphabetical order. As the man handed out diplomas he would say something about each graduate. When my name was called it was a proud moment for me. I walked across the stage to receive my diploma. Along with it I got an unexpected blow. "It is amazing that you've graduated," the man said. "You work hard, but you still will not amount to anything. If you can get a job, all you'll ever be is maybe a janitor." I was stunned. I blushed and walked back to my seat. I glanced at my mom and saw her in tears. My dad's face was flushed with anger. It seemed that everyone believed the handicapped were worthless. This kind of treatment, though, had always made me more determined to prove people wrong.

Like the other new graduates, I went job hunting after graduation. I didn't have any problem getting a job, thanks to my father and some of his friends who worked at the Cleveland Electric Illuminate Company. It was only a ten-minute walk from where we lived. I applied for a janitor position and was told to go to the company doctor in Cleveland to see if I was physically able to work. He checked me over and asked me, "How can you work if you can't hear well?"

"How do you think I understood what you just said? I read

lips," I replied.

"But you can't talk either."

"So what? I don't need to talk to do the cleaning." The doctor thought a moment and then passed me. I may have been only a janitor, but I was determined to show them what a handicapped person could do.

I reported for work the following Monday. The daily foreman showed me where the locker room was and gave me my locker assignment. After changing into my work clothes, I was given instructions on what needed to be done. I was to sweep daily, use the mopping machine twice a week, shine the brass, wash the windows, empty waste baskets, and whatever else needed to be done. None of this was hard for me because I had done the same chores at home for years. I worked a full eight-hour day with a half-hour for lunch. I worked lots of overtime when high company officials were coming to inspect the plant.

4

MATERIAL WEALTH AND SPIRITUAL POVERTY

Soon my hard work began to pay off. I saved my money and bought stocks, bonds, and property. I had a sizable bank account and became known as a smart businessman. I also liked to show off. When televisions became available, I paid $600 cash for a ten-inch black and white TV. I bought Mom, Dad, and myself the best clothing outfits that money could buy, and I always paid cash. I even bought my dad a new Nash automobile, again with cash. Of course, my money bought me many "friends" who hoped they could get something from me. I liked to take them all out to eat to show them what a wealthy young man I was.

My desire to be accepted as "one of the boys" led to my spiritual downfall. Temptation was all around me, and I took up smoking and drinking. Dad smoked and drank, and I thought if it was good enough for him, it was good enough for me. Mom was upset when Dad bought me my first pipe and pouch of tobacco. I thought I was a real man. The men at work did these things, and now I thought I could fit in with them. I even got involved in the plant bowling league. I became captain of a team that won the league championship.

All of this time I was still going to Avon Baptist Church. Rev. V. D. Geren, the man who had led me to Christ, had taken the pastorate of a church in Trenton, New Jersey. Later he bought some property and established the Shadyrest Bible Conference. The new pastor at Avon Baptist did not know me very well. I tried to put on a good show on Sunday. I once taught Sunday school. Their need for teachers was so great that they were willing to put up with my poor speaking ability. I even sang in the choir, even though there was no way that I as a deaf person could carry a tune.

All of my religious activity, however, didn't remove the guilt I felt in my heart. I knew I was a hypocrite, acting one way with

Christians on Sunday and another way with my worldly friends during the rest of the week. I thought I was fooling people at church, but they could smell the smoke on my clothing. Many of them began to pray for me. I knew for sure that I wasn't fooling God. I had all the things I thought would make me happy, and yet I was miserable.

SHADYREST BIBLE CONFERENCE

One day in early 1949, I got a message at work that someone was there who wanted to see me. *Now who would come here to see me?* I wondered as I walked through the door to the lobby with a cigarette dangling from my lips. To my horror, there was Pastor Geren! I ripped the cigarette out of my mouth and tried to hide it behind my back. He began to ask how I was getting along and made small talk. All this time the smoke was curling up around my ears, the ashes were falling, and the heat was increasing between my fingers! Finally he said, "Bill, you'd better put that thing out before you burn yourself." Here was the man who had led me to Christ, and he had caught me smoking literally red-handed. I had never been so embarrassed. He didn't say anything about it, however. He did invite me and Chuck Webb to his conference ground. I told him I wanted to come. "That's great, Bill. But I have to tell you, there won't be any smoking on the grounds."

"That's all right," I told him. "It's not a big thing to me. I can quit anytime."

Soon we were packed and traveling by train from Cleveland to Trenton, New Jersey. I had my cigarettes along. *I can quit anytime,* I told myself, *but they may come in handy.*

When we arrived at the depot in Trenton someone met us and took us to the Shadyrest Bible Conference in Chesterfield, which was ten miles from the depot. Shadyrest was different from any place I had ever known. Tall trees surrounded an old mansion that needed much repair. Chickens scratched about in the yard. An old army barracks served as the church, and there they had services. All of this was on five acres of land.

Chuck and I stayed in a little room at the back of the Geren's apartment. I liked it, and I thought I might enjoy coming back here to stay longer.

"We're not going to eat until after the evening service," said Rev. Geren. " I hope you can wait. We're going out for pizza."

Thinking I had misunderstood, I said, "We're going out for a piece of what?"

"Pizza pie," he answered.

I thought I could eat a lot more than just a piece of pie, but I didn't want to ask if we were getting anything else to eat. Instead I asked, "A piece of what kind of pie?"

Exasperated, he said, "Tomato pie!"

That sounded awful to me. "What kind of place would serve tomato pie?"

"An Italian place," he said as he went back out the door shaking his head.

All through the service I had no idea what was going on for I was trying to figure a way to get out of eating this awful tomato pie. When the service ended, I was hustled along into a car with the others and we headed for the Italian place. There was no way out. I made up my mind that I was going to have a hamburger even if I had to pay for it myself.

Going into the Italian cafe everything smelled good, but I couldn't enjoy it thinking about that tomato pie. "Bill," Pastor Geren said, "don't order anything until you have tried the pizza." I resented his ordering me around, but he was paying for the pizza. I resigned myself to waiting. After a while the waitress appeared carrying an odd round thing with tomato sauce, cheese, and onions in the middle of a crust. While Pastor Geren gave thanks I prayed the thing would disappear, but it didn't. Everyone dove into it except me. Pastor Geren looked at me. "What do you think, Bill?"

"I think it's too late," I replied. "Someone already ate it and couldn't hold it down." I did try it, and I had to admit that it was good.

Back at Shadyrest there were "No Smoking" signs all over the place. To have a smoke I had to sneak out behind the chicken coop or go for a walk on the grounds. I doubt I was fooling anyone, but nothing was said to me about it. Too soon the week passed, and it was time to go back home and back to work. I was surprised at how reluctant I was to leave Shadyrest.

FALLING IN LOVE WITH FLORIDA

I quickly got back into the routine of work, church, bowling, and living two lives. I was miserable, even with all the money I had in the bank.

My parents noticed my depression and thought a vacation would cheer me up. In March they decided we would take three weeks and go to Florida. I knew such a state existed, but I didn't know where it was. I only knew that it was far away. We left on a cold morning and headed south. I wore a sweater under my winter coat and a warm hat on my head. We traveled farther in one day than we had ever gone before and made it all the way to West Virginia. It was cold again when we left early the next morning , but as we headed south I noticed it was getting warmer. Off came my winter coat. We kept pushing south, stopping only for gas and food. Finally Dad said, "We made it!" I looked up and saw a sign that said, "Welcome to North Carolina." It was late, so we began to look for a place to spend the night. Dad pulled into a strange-looking place called a "motel."

"What is a motel?" I asked. "I know what a hotel is, but what is this?"

"This is something they have in the south," Mom told me. "It's like a hotel but with more rooms."

An old southern gentleman checked us in. After we took our luggage to our room it was time to eat. "Now we're going to enjoy some southern cooking," Mom announced. We found a restaurant and Mom did the ordering-Southern fried chicken, corn bread, mashed potatoes and gravy, turnip greens, and coffee. I had never eaten corn bread or turnip greens, but I liked them. Then for dessert we had banana pudding.

The next morning at breakfast I got another treat. Along with the ham and eggs was some white stuff that looked like sand. "What's this?" I asked Mom.

"They call it hominy grits, Bill. It's made from corn ground up real fine. You can put some of this red ham gravy over it. It's good."

I tried it, and it sure was good. I thought that I would like living in the south and eating southern cooking.

We journeyed on to our destination—Tallahassee, Florida. We stopped at a beautiful new motel with a swimming pool. I had never seen anything like it. We checked in, and when I heard the price of the rooms I exclaimed, "We only want to rent a room for one night, not buy it!" Everyone laughed, but I never knew that rooms could cost so much. Florida was a whole new world, and I loved every minute of my time there. We traveled all over the state. Soon it was time to leave for cold Ohio, but I wished I could stay in Florida. I hoped that maybe someday I could live there.

ONE MONTH TO LIVE

Soon I was back home in the same old routine with the same crowd. Time passed, and I continued to follow along with them, smoking, drinking, and getting into fights. Then on Sundays I went to church. There was no happiness in my double life. In the meantime my sisters had married, and soon I became "Uncle Bill." I liked that title, and I loved my nieces and nephews. I wanted to be married and have children of my own, but what girl would want to marry a man with afflictions? I became more depressed. Something was going to have to change, and that change was about to take place.

One morning in May 1951, I went to work although I felt tired and unwell. I just shook it off, thinking that I must be coming down with a cold or the flu. I picked up my time card and walked into the locker room to change into my work outfit.

The foreman saw me and asked, "What's the matter, Bill? You don't look good. You're as pale as a ghost. Are you sick?"

"I think I'm coming down with something," I told him. "I'll be all right." It was Friday, and I thought if I could just make it through the day I would have time to get better over the weekend.

I worked all morning doing my normal chores. At lunch one of my foremen stared at me. "Bill, you sure do look bad. I have an idea that you have more than just a cold. You ought to go on home."

"I will in three more hours," I said, still thinking it was flu or a cold coming on. I joked with the men and returned to work.

"Bill, those windows up there need cleaning. How about going up there and washing them?" the boss said. Those windows were about fifteen feet off the floor, and I disliked cleaning them. *They always need cleaning,* I thought. *They'll be dirty again in half an hour.* But he was the boss, so I got the ladder and filled a bucket with soapy water. I dipped my cleaning rag in the bucket, wrung out the excess water, and started climbing up to the ladder. Suddenly I felt dizzy. I climbed slowly, thinking it would pass, until I reached the top of the ladder. Then I blacked out.

I fell the fifteen feet to the concrete floor. My co-workers rushed over to me. I looked like I was dead, and a couple of these grown men wept. Then one of them realized I was still alive. "Call an ambulance," he cried. They covered me and tried to make me comfortable. Someone prayed. They didn't think I was going to make it.

Finally the ambulance arrived. Instead of taking me to the Lorain Hospital, they took me all the way to the Cleveland Clinic, for the boss wanted the best care possible for me. I remained unconscious while they worked on me.

I opened my eyes. *Where am I? Wait, I know this smell. I recognize this place. A hospital. But what happened? Why am I hooked up to these machines?* I had many more questions. Soon a nurse came in to my room. She noticed I had my eyes open.

"Hi! I'm glad to see you finally decided to wake up," she said cheerily. "In case you want to know, you're our guest at the Cleveland Clinic."

"What happened?" I croaked.

Her voice turned serious. "Mr. Maher, you had a bad fall at work yesterday and scared everyone. Now don't try to talk. The doctor will be here to see you as soon as he can. Your parents are outside waiting to see you. Would you like to see them for a few minutes? Just nod your head." I nodded. *Why was I so weak?*

Mom and Dad came in with bloodshot eyes, looking tired. They both looked as though they had been crying. Mom began fussing over me, cooing, "You're going to be fine. Everything is all right. You'll be back home in no time." Dad just stood looking at me and shaking his head. *Now I'm really starting to worry. It was more than just a fall. I must be in pretty bad shape.* Somehow I knew that my life would never be the same.

Finally a doctor came in. He was all business and coldly professional. "Well, young man," he began, "I'm surprised you have survived. You probably don't realize it, but you had a heart attack. Actually, you have had several of them. I have never known anyone to survive what you have. The bad news is you probably have only a month to live. I suggest you get your house in order and enjoy the time you have left. I'll let you go home in a couple of days." Tears began to flow from Mom's and Dad's eyes. The doctor turned and walked out.

I was shocked. Did I understand right? *What does he mean I have only a month to live? It can't be true! I still haven't reached my twenty-third birthday. I've got my whole life ahead of me.* The nurse returned. "You'll have to go now," she said to my parents. "You can visit him again tomorrow." Mom kissed me and waved good-bye as she backed toward the door.

Now I was alone with my thoughts. I was facing death. Why did I have to have those heart attacks? Wasn't it enough that I was afflicted? Why should I have to suffer more? I realized I would soon face the God Who had saved me by His grace at the age of twelve. It bothered me that there were sins in my life, but I did not feel I needed to confess them. After all, I went to church. I had sung in the choir and taught Sunday school.

True to his word, the doctor let me go home after a couple of days. Before I left he handed me a bottle of white pills. "These pills contain nitroglycerin," he said. "Be sure to take one if you feel like you are going to have another heart attack. Just put one under your tongue. You have a month's supply which should be enough, but let me know if you need more. Just do whatever you feel like doing, or go on a trip. Try to enjoy the time you have left."

REDEDICATION

This doctor sure didn't help my feelings. How was I supposed to enjoy myself when I had only a month to live? I decided I would visit the man who had led me to Christ. I wrote to Rev. Geren and told him about my condition. I asked him if I could spend a couple of weeks with his family before I died. He wrote back to say he would be glad to have me come.

Rev. Geren was holding meetings at a Baptist church in Strongsville, Ohio. We made plans for me to arrive on the Friday, the last night of his meetings. Then I would travel all night with them back to Shadyrest.

My parents loaded my luggage and we left Avon Lake. We arrived in Strongsville in the pouring rain. Dad finally found the church. We turned in and a retarded man was there to direct us to the parking lot. Even with his limitations he was doing all he could to serve the Lord faithfully, regardless of the weather. I felt ashamed because I wasn't doing anything for Christ.

After the service we loaded our luggage into the trunk of the Geren's car, had a snack, and took off about 11 p.m. for the long ride to Chesterfield, New Jersey. I fell asleep in the back seat and didn't awaken until we stopped for breakfast just before we reached Shadyrest.

I stayed in the same back room of the Geren's house I had stayed in before. My parents were coming for me in two weeks, and I determined I would do all I could before they arrived. I didn't bring any cigarettes with me this time.

I ate all my meals with the Gerens. When they gave thanks for the food they always mentioned my name. Every night I heard messages that brought me under increasing conviction. Here I was facing death with sin in my life. I felt ashamed to face my Savior Who loved me and gave Himself for me. I began to confess my sins, great and small, to the Lord. By the middle of the second week I had settled everything with the Lord. How wonderful to know He not only forgives sins, according to I John 1:8-10, but it was also a comfort to read in Hebrews 8:12 and 10:17-18 that He forgets sins. I surrendered my life to do whatever He wanted me to do with the days I had remaining.

I told Rev. Geren about my decision, and he put me to work right away. I worked with the young people, and I helped in practical ways by cleaning the yard and taking care of the Geren children, Larry and Carol. I asked the Gerens if I could stay with them the rest of the summer—that is, if I lived that long. Rev. Geren said I could stay, and if I dropped dead he would ship my body back home.

"Fine," I said. "I don't want it anyway."

CALLED TO THE MINISTRY

I felt I needed to quit my job and go full time in the Lord's work, but what or where I did not know. Two verses, II Corinthians 5:8 and I John 3:2, became very precious to me. Not only do they promise eternity with Christ, but they also teach that the afflicted will one day be like Christ and thus no longer have their afflictions.

My mother and father came to take their twenty-three-year-old son back home to die, but to their surprise I told them I wasn't going home. I told them I had given myself to the Lord and I was going to quit my job. They begged me to wait until September, for they were sure I would get over this foolishness and go back to my job if I should live. My dad was angry, and my mom was in tears. We said our good-byes, and they went back to Avon Lake believing they would never again see me alive. They expected me to come home in a box.

I soon learned that "Shadyrest" was a misnomer, for I worked as hard as ever. I coined a saying, "All shade and no rest!" The Bible conferences ended, fall arrived, and I was still alive. I asked Rev. Geren if I could stay the rest of the year. "Yes, Bill, but only on one condition. You have to begin preparing for the ministry the Lord has for you."

"What ministry?" I said, confused. "I'm satisfied with what the Lord is doing with me now."

"I think God is calling you to preach, Bill. Many have heard your testimony here this summer, and I think God has more for you to do," he said.

I couldn't help but laugh. "What about my speech? No one can understand me. It took you the whole summer to figure out what I was saying."

Rev. Geren didn't reply. He left the room and returned with a tape recorder and microphone. He told me to practice my speech, so every day I used the tape recorder for two or three hours. People began to understand me better. I found myself preaching in churches, rescue missions, and on street corners. Souls were saved. People were getting right with God. I was surprised, but God wasn't.

My parents had become concerned about me. I had told them I was going to go into a full-time preaching ministry. My father got angry. He would rather have a son who was a janitor than one who was a preacher. He told me I couldn't even come home to visit. I was a very lonely fellow.

After a while I moved up to the third floor of the old mansion. I began helping Rev. Geren build a house in back of the mansion. Every day we got up early in the morning and worked until late at night.

One Friday evening, Rev. Geren said he wanted to sleep late on Saturday. I was all for it. The next morning I heard someone yelling for me from the second story. I went from my room on the third floor to see who it was. "It's a long distance from Washington, D. C.," said Rev. Geren. I put on my bathrobe and walked all the way down to the first floor wondering who would call me from Washington, D. C. I picked up the phone, and the operator said, "Number, please." No one was calling.

Puzzled, I hung up and there Rev. Geren stood with a mischievous grin. "I thought you said it was a long distance from Washington, D. C.," I said to him.

"Yes, it is 175 miles from Washington, D. C. to here," he replied. "I didn't say anything about a phone call. I just mentioned that it was a long distance between here and there. But now that we're both up, Bill, let's eat breakfast and go to work on the house. I couldn't sleep, and it looks like you couldn't either."

"What do you mean? I was sleeping well until you started yelling. In fact, I could still go back to sleep."

"Now, Bill, that wouldn't be good. We could finish the house today." He grabbed my arm and pulled me toward the table. It's a good thing I loved this guy because I could have killed him. Before breakfast was over, however, I was laughing at the good joke Rev. Geren pulled on me.

5

BEGINNING MY MINISTRY

I continued to search the Scriptures and grow in the Lord. I wanted to know the Lord's will for my life. During my daily devotions I read II Corinthians 1:3-4. These verses speak of "the God of all comfort, who comforteth us in all our tribulation, that we may be able to comfort them which are in any trouble, by the comfort wherewith we ourselves are comforted of God." God was using these verses to call me into His work. It was as though God was saying, "I have comforted you in your afflictions all these years. Now it is time for you to comfort others. I want you to preach wherever I send you." It seemed that God wanted me in evangelism, especially to the afflicted.

When I came to II Corinthians 12, I saw that Paul, too, had an affliction. I wondered if Luke, a physician, accompanied Paul because of his affliction. Paul prayed for God to heal him, but God said no. Instead, He gave him grace to bear his affliction. In I Corinthians 15:10 Paul said although he was what he was by the grace of God, he also worked harder than anyone else for God. I was used to hard work. My handicaps required me to work harder than "normal" people just to learn how to do things most of them took for granted. Besides, Paul said in Philippians 4:13, "I can do all things through Christ which strengtheneth me." So could I.

God was removing all of my objections to His call. Still, I argued with the Lord and reminded Him that I had a speech impediment. Of course, He hadn't forgotten. He directed me to Exodus 4:10-12 where Moses made the same objections I was making, and God reminded Moses that He was the One Who had made him that way. Of all the men God could have used, He picked Moses, who could not talk right. God defeated all my arguments. I took Exodus 4:12 as a promise and started out. "Now therefore go, and I will be with thy mouth, and teach thee what

45

thou shalt say,"

I moved into the Gerens' basement, but I wanted to support myself as much as I could. When I got no invitations to someone's house for a meal, I went down to the basement and had bread and water. I frequently preached at Unionville Bible Church and at Trenton Rescue Mission, but no money came in. I still had money in the bank back in Ohio. God spoke to my heart about giving this money to His work through Luke 18:18-24, but I argued with Him. I can live on it until I can get some money coming in, I reasoned. It seemed the Lord was saying, "You have proven what a handicapped man can do. Now I want to show the world what I can do with a handicapped man." *Okay, Lord.* I invested the money in the Lord's work.

I managed to get a Model T Ford truck and I started selling eggs in Trenton and Bordentown, New Jersey. At first I would bid on the dozens of eggs at the Columbus Auction and sell them at a profit. Finally I found a farmer who would sell me all the eggs I wanted directly. If any eggs got broken, I took them home to eat. I ate eggs poached, fried, and scrambled. I ate omelets. I ate eggs, eggs, and more eggs.

My old Model T was held together with wire. If I had to wait at a red light the radiator would overheat. I always had to carry extra water with me. I finally traded it for an English Ford with no heater, a necessity in cold New Jersey. Ger, the family's name for Rev. Geren, suggested I punch a hole in the floor to let in some heat from the engine.

Christmas was approaching. I wanted to go home to see my parents, but my dad had said I couldn't come home. I decided to try it anyway. Maybe I could sneak in the back door while he was at work.

I took off for Avon Lake, Ohio, in my English Ford with no heater except for a hole in the floor. I wrapped my legs in blankets, but it was so cold I had to stop periodically to walk around and get the circulation going again in my legs. I finally arrived at my parents' house. I plowed through the snow around to the back door, and there stood my dad.

"What are you doing here?" he shouted. "Didn't I tell you

you couldn't come home?"

I gulped, my heart aching. "I haven't seen you and Mom for two years. I thought it was time for me to spend Christmas with you."

He hesitated a moment. "Well, since you're here, you might as well stay until after New Year's." He swung the door open and I went in. Mom was glad, and Dad really was too. He was just too proud to admit it.

While in Avon Lake I checked with area pastors to see if I could have a ministry among the handicapped. I wanted to start a church or have a weekly service for them. No one was interested, except Dr. Ralph Neighbor at the Church of the Open Door in Elyria. He said he would be glad to have me. I told him I would get back in touch with him after I moved back to Ohio. I was sure my dad wouldn't want me living with him, so I had to find a place to live. I had to get a different car, and I needed money to live on.

My parents were aware of my need for a car and offered to buy me a used Nash Rambler. I told them they didn't need to do that, but Dad reminded me that I had bought him a brand new Nash a few years before; so I allowed them to buy it for me. I was very thankful that it had a good heater, and the seats could be folded down to make a bed. God had taken care of one of my biggest needs. God was taking care of some other needs as well.

One day I decided to visit some of my former co-workers down at the electric plant. To my surprise, they told me that Dad frequently bragged about his son the preacher and told them all the things I was doing. When Dad got home from work, I asked him about this. He scowled and asked, "Who told you this?"

"Oh, the fellows at the plant," I answered.

"Those guys always did talk too much," said the one who supposedly didn't want anyone to know I was a preacher.

I soon got another surprise. Dad asked if I wanted to move back home when I started my ministry to the handicapped. I made him repeat it two or three times. I couldn't believe what I was hearing. Now God had solved two of my problems. The only one that remained was the money.

While I was staying with my parents, I visited Avon Baptist Church where I was saved. The new pastor, Rev. Gerald Mitchell, asked if I would be willing to preach on Sunday. I gladly accepted. All my old church friends were there. Mom even came, and I really enjoyed preaching that day. Then they gave me a love offering, the first one I had ever received. God was taking care of my last problem. Rev. Mitchell became a friend, and he arranged for me to preach at several other churches. Soon it was time to head back to Shadyrest. Ger and Harriet were glad to see me. They were thrilled at how God had given me a new car and provided for my needs, and had given me opportunities to preach.

God Won't Use a Quitter

Ger and Harriet were glad to see me. They were thrilled at how God had given me a new car and provided for my needs, and given me opportunities to preach.

I began to make plans to move back to Ohio to start my ministry to the handicapped. Somehow I had to get meetings in churches to let people know about the work the Lord wanted me to do. I was happy, then, when a I got a letter from the pastor of Conneautville Baptist Church in Conneautville, Pennsylvania, asking me to preach one Sunday in February. I had been there once before when Ger preached a week of meetings, but now the church had a different pastor.

I didn't have enough money with me to buy food and pay for gas and tolls, but it shouldn't have been a problem since I assumed I would be invited to eat with someone and I would receive a love offering. I would take some bread with me to eat on the way and save my money to buy gas and pay the tolls on the Pennsylvania Turnpike.

I arrived at the pastor's house about supper time on Saturday evening. The pastor answered the door. I introduced myself, and he said, "You're not to be here until tomorrow morning." He shut the door without another word. I was dumbfounded. Here I was with no place to eat or stay. The weather wasn't all that was cold here, I decided.

I went back to my car. My feelings were hurt. I drove until I found a gas station. I asked if I could park there for the night, and he said I could. He added that he closed at 10 p.m., but he would leave me the restroom key so I could use the restroom the next day when he would be closed all day. By now I was so hungry I had a headache. I ate some bread, folded the seats down in the car, and covered up with my winter coat.

When morning came, I used the gas station restroom to wash and get ready for church. I ate more bread and drank water from the tap. I still thought I had better save my money. Surely after church someone would invite me for a meal and then my headache would go away.

After I taught Sunday school and preached in the morning service, I stood with the pastor by the front door. I shook hands with people as they left. I kept hoping someone would ask me to dinner, but no one did. When everyone was gone the pastor said, "See you tonight at the youth meeting and the evening service."

I trudged back to my car and had another slice of bread. I said to myself, *When I get that love offering tonight, I'm going to find a restaurant and get the biggest steak they have.*

I drove back to the gas station and took a nap in my car. I returned to the church at 6 p.m. for the youth meeting. My headache was worse than ever. I spoke to the teens and preached in the evening service. No love offering was taken at the end of the service. Afterward the pastor came over to me. I assumed he was going to give me a gift. "You've done a good job today," he said. "If you ever need a place to preach, you are welcome here." He turned and left.

I stormed out to my car. My head was pounding. I had only enough money to get home. I was so angry I drove all night. All the way back to Shadyrest I kept repeating, "I quit! No more preaching if that's how I will be treated."

I arrived early in the morning, ate the last of my bread, and went to sleep. At noon Ger woke me up to ask how the meetings went. I gave him an earful, griping about how badly I had been treated. He just listened. At last I whined, "If that's the way people are going to treat me, I quit!"

Ger stood up and said quietly, "Go ahead and quit. Be a quitter. God cannot and will not use a quitter." He turned and walked out. No sympathy, no nothing. I was furious! But deep down I knew Ger was right. The Holy Spirit began to deal with me and showed me I was really mad at God for not taking care of me the way I thought I should be taken care of. I confessed my sin of griping, and God soon put me to the test.

A short time later a letter arrived from the new pastor at Conneautville Baptist Church. He asked me to come to preach again. *Oh, no,* I groaned. I asked God to give me grace and told Him I would go and be thankful for the opportunity to preach even if I received nothing.

When I arrived, the pastor apologized for what had happened before. They took care of me and gave me a love offering. I was on cloud nine all the way back to Shadyrest, praising God for His faithfulness. They also became my first supporting church, at ten dollars a month. If I had still been angry and refused to go back I would have missed God's blessing. He was teaching me to trust Him.

SHADYREST ADVENTURES

I continued to work at Shadyrest between meetings, which led to all kinds of adventures. The Lord was looking out for me though. One time Ger asked me to cut a big tree limb that was touching the roof. The ladder reached to the limb, and I tied the ladder to the limb above the place where I would be sawing. Ger yelled up at me, "You don't need to do that. The ladder won't move." I did it anyway. The last time I had fallen from a ladder I had almost died. I went up the ladder and cut that big limb. It fell to the ground, but without the weight of the limb the tree trunk suddenly straightened and jerked my ladder off the ground. I hung on for dear life as the ladder swung back and forth. If I hadn't tied the ladder, it surely would have fallen.

Another time we noticed the roof was leaking during a rain storm. When the rain ended, we checked the roof and noticed some slates were missing. Ger asked me to go up and replace them, so up on the roof I went. I soon learned that leather shoes were the wrong thing to wear on a wet slate roof! As I crawled along three stories off the ground, I began to slide toward the edge. *Lord, I'm coming home!* I thought this was the end.

Just as I reached the edge, my clothing caught on two nails that were sticking up. I gingerly removed my shoes and carefully crawled back to the dormer window. When the roof was dry, I tied a rope around my waist and anchored it around the chimney. This time I fixed the roof and did it right.

Then there was the time Ger decided we needed some horses. We figured we had to have a corral, but neither of us had any idea how to build one. There was a fellow named John Lane staying with us at Shadyrest, and he said to put up some posts and nail boards around the outside of the posts. It sounded good to us, so that's how we did it. Ger put a couple of horses in our corral, and everything was fine until we had a thunderstorm one night.

By this time I was wearing a hearing aid, so when Ger beat on my door I woke up. He yelled, "Bill, the horses are gone. Come help me find them." I put on my shoes, and out we went with our flashlights. Apparently the horses had become frightened during the storm, and they had pushed the boards away from the posts and escaped. We fixed the fence before going after the horses. We found one and herded it into the corral, and began hunting for the other one. After about an hour the horse ran by me headed toward Ger. "He's coming your way," I yelled. I watched his flashlight do a flip, so I ran over to him. He was lying on the wet ground laughing.

"What happened?" I asked. "I saw your flashlight go flying."

Ger was laughing so hard it took a minute before he could speak. "When the horse got to me I grabbed his tail as he went by and held on. I did a flip along with the flashlight." Now we were both laughing. We finally found the horse and put it back in the corral.

The next day we took off all the boards from the outside of the posts and nailed them to the inside so the horses couldn't push them off. I had lost my hearing aid looking for the horses.

We spent a lot of time looking for it, but never found it. I noticed, however, that I could hear pretty well without it, and we all thanked the Lord for my hearing.

MINISTERING IN OHIO

In the summer of 1954 it was time for me to move back home to Avon Lake to begin my ministry there. I loaded all my earthly possessions into my car. Shadyrest had been my home, so it was with many tears that I said good-bye to the Gerens and others.

My parents were glad to have me back home. I moved into my old room. At least I will be well-fed, I thought.

I started inviting all the handicapped I could to our first church meeting at the Church of the Open Door in Elyria. Dr. Ralph Neighbor was very gracious in allowing me to use a room with a piano. These Christians knew the truth of John 9:1-4, where Jesus explains that a man was born blind so that He could do His work through the man. They realized that God had made these afflicted people for a purpose. They were able to look beyond a person's affliction and see a soul for whom Christ died.

My sister, Lenore Eastin, played the piano for us. I would attend the morning service at Avon Baptist Church, drive to Elyria for our meeting from 2 p.m. until 4 p.m. on Sunday afternoon, and drive back to Avon Baptist for the evening service. We never had a special name for our group. We just called it a church. Deaf people, blind people, people with all kinds of afflictions attended. Our group grew, and later we even had a blind piano player.

The afflicted readily identified with a Savior who was "touched with the feeling of our infirmities" (Hebrews 4:15). I pointed out to them that some were born afflicted so that Jesus could show His power through them, like the blind man in John 9. I also pointed them to II Corinthians 12, where Paul talks about his own affliction. At first Paul complained and asked God to remove his infirmity, but God revealed to Paul that His grace is sufficient, and that His strength is perfected in our weakness (v. 9).

UNSAVED FAMILY MEMBERS

I was having a great time preaching, but at the same time I was becoming increasingly concerned about my unsaved family members. I prayed for them and witnessed to them as often as I could. Dad would get mad and yell, "Get off my back!" I led Lenore's husband, Bill Eastin, to the Lord. Dorothy had moved to Arizona before I returned home. I tried to witness to her by writing letters, but she never wrote back. Finally I stopped writing and prayed that God would send someone to witness to them. All the while I kept working on Dad.

One day Dad was down in the basement when Mom and I heard him fall and yell for help. I ran down the stairs as fast as my legs would carry me. Dad was lying on the floor bleeding from around his eyes. His glasses had broken and cut his face. I weighed all of 128 pounds, but somehow I carried Dad's 210 pounds upstairs. I laid him on the floor and covered him while Mom called the ambulance. Then I called Lenore to take Mom to the hospital. I wanted to ride with Dad in the ambulance.

Soon the ambulance came and Dad was loaded in. As they worked on Dad, I was sure he would die before we reached the hospital.

"Dad, I don't know if you're going to make it. You are bleeding badly. Dad, where will you go if you die?"

"Hell," he answered.

"Do you want to go there?" I asked.

"No."

"Do you want to get saved and be sure you will go to heaven?"

"Yes," he whispered. Then it was my privilege to lead my 68-year-old dad to Christ.

We arrived at the hospital. Dad was taken into the emergency room while I waited and prayed with Mom and Lenore. Two hours later Dad was wheeled out in a wheelchair with a smile on his face and a big bandage on his eye.

"He sure is a lucky man," the doctor said. "The glass just cut his eye lid. Those cuts always bleed a lot. Take him home and bring him back next week."

As we rode back home, I asked, "Dad, what happened to you in the ambulance?"

He smiled. "I received Christ as my Savior. I really did it." I didn't say anything then, but I had hurt my back carrying him up the stairs. It would hurt me for years to come, but it was worth it to have the privilege of leading my dad to Christ.

Soon the Lord began to burden me to reach the handicapped in Pennsylvania and New Jersey. I decided to return to Shadyrest and make it my headquarters from which I would preach as the Lord opened doors. Before I left I wanted to make sure my Christian friends were settled in good, Bible-believing Baptist churches. I did not want any of them going to liberal churches that did not believe and preach the Word of God. We had a farewell party, and it was a sad time.

WESTON AND BOB

Before I moved I took my old friend Weston Charleston with me to our Wednesday night prayer meeting. It was the first time he had ever been to a Baptist church. When it was time to pray, we knelt between the pews, unlike they did at his Methodist church. Weston managed to get his 250-pound bulk stuck down there between the pews. He was quietly trying to get my attention to help him, but I had my eyes closed praying. After all, I was talking to the Lord, and surely he understood that he shouldn't interrupt someone praying.

I finally said "Amen" and saw Weston's pitiful condition. His face was red, from embarrassment or exertion, I couldn't tell which. "I'm stuck. Help me up!" he pleaded. I couldn't help but laugh at the whole situation, which made poor Weston mad. I tried to pull him and push him, but he wouldn't budge. By this time people were staring, I was laughing, and Weston was mad enough to kill me.

Then a hero showed up with a screwdriver. He started unscrewing the screws that held the pew to the floor. We moved the pew and Weston was free. He left church as fast as he could. For some reason I never could get him to come back to Avon Baptist

Church with me.

Some time later I visited him, and we both laughed about it. Weston had married a deaf girl who had been in Mrs. Spoerl's class with us, and he told her about getting stuck with me in church.

Once when I visited them I heard their baby cry in the next room of their second-floor apartment. Weston's wife said, "Excuse me, my baby's crying."

"Weston, how does she know that? If a bomb went off outside your house, neither of you would be able to hear it."

"I don't know, Bill," he replied. "Maybe she can feel a slight vibration, or maybe it's just a mother's intuition." I never cease to be amazed at what handicapped people can do.

I also visited with another old childhood friend, Bob McNally. Bob called me on the phone and said he had permission from the Pope to visit with me for five minutes. He did not know I had become a Baptist preacher. I had heard he was studying to become a Catholic priest, but I was in for a surprise. When his sister drove him over I went out to meet him. Instead of being a priest, Bob had become a monk and now lived in Texas. He was dressed in a black robe, with a rope for a belt, and leather sandals. His head was shaved bald.

I welcomed Bob into the house and got him comfortably seated. "Bob," I said, "you need to be born again. You need to accept Christ as your Savior."

Bob was horrified by my words. "Did you become a Baptist preacher like you said you would when we were kids?"

"Yes," I said, "but really I am a born-again preacher." I spent the next few minutes telling him that he was a sinner and needed to be saved.

"I've done everything I can to atone for my sins," he protested. "I have walked on glass, whipped my back, and suffered hunger and all kinds of discomfort. I even shaved my head so I wouldn't have pride. What more can I do?"

"Bob, it's already done by Jesus Christ on the cross of Calvary by His death, burial, and resurrection. Christ said, 'It is finished!' "

Bob jumped up and said he had to go. "I've got to do more," he mumbled as he ran out of the house. I was very sad for Bob, who was trying to earn his way to heaven. The Bible tells us that this is impossible, and that all we need to do is accept by faith God's free gift of salvation.

6

BACK TO SHADYREST

In the fall of 1955 I moved back to Shadyrest, my second home. I was happy to be back with my friends there. We all had to catch up on news about what God had been doing in our lives. I had plans to make, and after praying about it I decided to visit Rev. Bob Matthew in Wilkes-Barre, Pennsylvania, and see what the Lord might have in mind for me in that area.

The Lord soon burdened my heart for the handicapped around Wilkes-Barre and Scranton. I settled in at the Y. M. C. A. in Carbondale during the week and returned to Shadyrest on the weekends. On Wednesday evenings I attended Rev. Matthew's church, and sometimes he let me preach.

After I had been in this new area for a while, I had preaching opportunities at churches in Waymart, South Clinton, and Honesdale. I made the rounds to visit various ones who were handicapped. Once I met one afflicted person, others were easy to find for they often knew one another from being in special schools or hospitals together. These people were wonderful to meet. I often stopped to visit the men at the Veterans' Hospital in Wilkes-Barre on my way to the Matthews' house for supper. They were glad to have someone visit them, even if he was a missionary.

I once stopped at the home of a family that had a handicapped child. I introduced myself and the mother invited me in.

"You sit down at the kitchen table and try some of my chili and homemade bread," she ordered. She didn't have to tell me twice. I sat down and she served me the food and a glass of iced tea.

I dug in. "How do you like it?" she asked.

"It's delicious!" I replied.

The lady beamed. "Now what was it you wanted, Mr. Maher?" Just then her handicapped daughter came in and sat at the table.

I told them I was a Baptist preacher who ministered to the afflicted.

"I knew you were okay!" she exclaimed. "But we are Catholic. Is that all right?"

"Fine," I said. "I only want to tell about what Jesus Christ has done and what you can do to be saved." I figured it didn't make any difference if someone is a Catholic or Protestant; if that person doesn't know Christ as Savior, he or she is still a lost person. I gave them the gospel, and the whole time the afflicted daughter was watching and listening. They did not accept Christ that day, but later that year the whole family was saved-the father, the mother, the afflicted daughter, and two other children.

Another time someone mentioned a handicapped woman who was an alcoholic and played piano in a bar. She lost her legs one night when she got drunk and passed out on the train tracks. A train came by and severed her legs. The first time I visited her home, her husband laughed at me when I told them about Christ. But the woman didn't laugh.

I continued to visit her, and some time later she received Christ as her Savior. The next time I stopped in, the husband met me at the door with a shotgun.

"Because of you my wife doesn't drink anymore, and she quit her job at the bar. I'm going to kill you!"

God gave me the courage to shout back, "Go ahead. Then I'll be with Christ and I won't be afflicted anymore. And I won't have to work and pay taxes."

That gave him something to think about. "Well, I guess I'll let you live so you'll have to suffer with the rest of us."

7

FLORIDA BECKONS

In 1956 I was asked to move to the Harmony Heart Camp in Salisbury, North Carolina, operated by Brother and Mrs. Percy Smith. There I met several preachers who took part in the ministry of the camp. One was Rev. Bob Hess. I had been preaching for some time in area churches when Rev. Hess called and asked me to hold tent revival meetings in Salisbury that would last up to a month.

During one week, I had the opportunity to speak on the radio. Being on the radio gave me the idea to start a radio program just for the afflicted. For a short time I was on WPEL in Montrose, Pennsylvania. I called my program "The Courage and Hope Hour." Bill Ohman was my announcer, and his sister Ruth played the organ. Both were a big help. The handicapped, however, could not help pay for radio time, so I had to stop the program. I didn't give up on the idea, though.

In January of 1957 Rev. Geren invited me to hold joint meetings with him in Ocala, Florida. The meetings would go for two weeks at the Central Baptist Church where Rev. Walter Faust was the pastor. We had a blessed time, and to my amazement they asked me to return and start a work among the afflicted in Ocala.

From Ocala we went to Bradenton, Florida, to hold meetings at Calvary Baptist Church. The pastor, Dr. D. E. Luttrell, was an old friend, and he encouraged me to do the Lord's work in Ocala. It was only 150 miles from his church, and he said he would have me back for meetings and encourage other pastors to have me.

Ever since that family vacation to Florida years ago, I had wanted to live in Florida. But I really wanted to make sure that this was what the Lord wanted me to do. As a sign I asked the Lord to provide four things: a place to live, food for my stomach, gas for the car, and the names of four handicapped people. I knew from experience that just four handicapped people could put me in touch with dozens of others. Before a week had passed, God had answered every request. Somehow I knew that I would settle here the rest of my life.

I returned to Shadyrest to pack up once more. In March came the sad day when I again had to leave old friends, not just at Shadyrest, but also in all the towns and cities in Pennsylvania where I had ministered.

I drove to Sparr, Florida, near Ocala, where Mr. Albert Griggs owned a lumber business. He put me up in a motel until we could find a suitable place to live. I had very little money. My monthly support from Shadyrest and Conneautville Baptist Church totaled forty dollars.

After resting a couple of days, I set out to visit the four people whose names I had obtained in January. From each one I got other names. Within a short time I was very busy with a full-time ministry to the handicapped in Marion County, and especially in Ocala. Central Baptist was my home church, and Pastor Faust gave me the privilege of preaching there. He often had me over for meals, as did several other families in the church, and was always a great encouragement to me.

One thing I learned in a hurry was that dinner was not the evening meal like it was up North. Rather, it was at noon. The first time I was invited to be with a certain family from church at dinner, I showed up at 5 p.m. I rapped on the door only to be faced by an angry housewife.

"Where have you been? We waited and waited for you and finally decided to go ahead with the meal."

"You said you wanted me for dinner," I explained.

"You Yankees!" she exclaimed. "You don't get your language right. Dinner is at noon. Supper is in the evening." After my scolding, she invited me in and fed me a delicious meal. They had me over often, and I never made that mistake again.

I soon found a place to live at Berachah Colony, a great Christian work among alcoholics run by Andy and Betty Stiples. They let me live in an empty building, and I could eat with the men if I would work with the alcoholics along with the handicapped. I didn't think there was much difference between the two groups. To me the alcoholics just had a different kind of affliction.

ORDINATION

Churches opened their doors to me in Jacksonville, Bradenton, and Sarasota, as well as in Ocala. The Lord kept me busy preaching until that summer when I received an unexpected letter from Rev. Geren. He requested that I prepare for ordination. Me? Ordained? Be called Rev. William Thomas Maher? I never thought this would be possible for me as a handicapped person. I was pleased and excited at the prospect.

In June I returned to Shadyrest. I began studying for my ordination which was to take place over the Labor Day weekend. Rev. Geren's plan was to assemble an ordination council made up of area pastors. If I passed their examination, I would be ordained on Labor Day. The last Bible conference began on that weekend, and I would be the final speaker on the following Friday. While I studied I also helped out with the work at Shadyrest and did a little preaching.

One morning in August a young couple drove into our parking lot. I saw them from my apartment window, and I went down to meet them and show them around. I really wasn't paying attention when they told me their names. I along with everyone else assumed they were married. My mind was preoccupied with study for my ordination. I had to pass the test of the council.

At last the time came. The pastors questioned me on Saturday, and again on Sunday. I had never heard of anyone being questioned two days. Because my ministry to the afflicted was a new type of work, they had many questions. They also wanted to make sure that I was not going to get involved in the healing business. I said to the council, "I am concerned about one thing: getting people saved. If a person gets saved, when he sees Jesus he will be like Him, according to I John 3:2. We waste our time worrying about our bodies rather than our souls. Our bodies will die, but our souls will live somewhere forever. Those who are saved will get a perfect body like Christ's. The lost will be in hell to suffer apart from Him."

My parents arrived on Sunday. My ordination council announced their decision. I passed! What a relief! The ordination would take place the next day, on Labor Day. At last I was able to sleep peacefully.

The next day I watched as some people were baptized in the swimming pool on the conference grounds. I looked over, and there sitting next to me was the young couple I had shown around the grounds. Soon the fellow stood up and walked away.

"Where's your husband going?" I asked the woman.

"Husband? He's not my husband! I've never been married." She laughed. "I was wondering why everyone kept calling me Mrs. Barney. My name is Elizabeth June Barney, but people call me Betty."

Hmm. Not married. Interesting. I fired one question after another at this beautiful young lady. I figured I only had that week to get to know her so I had to work fast.

"Where do you live?" I asked.

"I share an apartment with my mother in Trenton, but I was born and reared in Wilkes-Barre, Pennsylvania," she said.

"What do you do?"

"I have a good job at Lenox Pottery. The company is famous for making dishes for the White House and other government offices. I inspect the dishes to ensure the quality."

"Are you saved?" I inquired.

"Yes, I was saved on July 17. The pastor at the Assembly of God church led me to Christ. When I saw a man preaching on the street in Trenton, I introduced myself and told him I had just been saved. He was Pastor Bob Matthews, and he asked me to come out here to hear him preach. He said it was only ten miles from where I live and he gave me directions, so here I am."

Betty asked her pastor about Shadyrest only to be told not to go there, for they preached "damnable doctrine." "They believe everyone can know they are saved," he told her. But she found this fellow to bring her out here anyway.

That night I was ordained. My parents were proud, and I was relieved to have it all behind me. I was the first person ever to be ordained at the Shadyrest Bible Conference.

A WHIRLWIND COURTSHIP

After the service I stood by the back door shaking hands with folks as they left. When I shook Betty's hand, she gave me an envelope. I put it in my coat pocket without looking inside.

We then went to the Gerens' house for refreshments and fellowship. At last everyone left, and I went to my room tired but rejoicing. I crawled in bed before I remembered the envelope from Betty. I dug it out of my coat pocket and opened it. She had enclosed fifty dollars and a short letter. She said the money was for me to get back home after this last week of meetings. She also said she had some questions about spiritual things and wanted to know if I could help her. *Great!* I thought. *I'll talk to her after I preach tomorrow night.* I fell asleep that night a very excited fellow.

The next day I could hardly wait until the services started that evening. Betty arrived with that same fellow. She apparently depended on him to bring her. Well, he may bring her, but I made up my mind that I was going to take her home.

After the service was over I hurried to the back door to shake hands with the people as they left. When Betty came near, I shook her hand and thanked her for her gift. "I understand you have some questions you would like me to answer," I said. "Would you like to talk tonight?"

"Yes," she replied. I wondered what the fellow with her would do. I wished he would just go away. I said to him, "There's a missionary film being shown in the house. Why don't you go in and watch it?" He mumbled something and stalked off toward the house.

"Let's sit outside where we can talk," I said to Betty. She thought that was a very good idea. We could see the moon and stars. It was a perfect set-up, except she really did have some good questions about the Christian life.

"How can we really know for sure that we are saved?" she asked. I showed her many verses from God's Word that prove a person can know he or she is saved.

"What's wrong with opera?" was her next question.

"You've got to be kidding," I said. "There's nothing wrong with opera." I have to admit that I did not enjoy opera. They sounded to me like they were screaming instead of singing. Instead of dropping dead when they were stabbed, they sang for half an hour. I never knew of anyone to sing when they were dying. But I didn't mention any of this, for I wanted to impress her with my sophisticated taste in music.

"What's wrong with women wearing make-up?" I knew this was out of my league.

"Let's go inside and you can ask Mrs. Geren," I suggested. Just then the fellow came back out. I knew I had to do something quick.

"It's going to take some time to answer all of Betty's questions," I told him. "Why don't you go on home and I'll take Betty home later." Betty agreed, but I could tell the fellow didn't like any of this.

I strolled with Betty into the house. We sat down with the Gerens, and Mrs. Geren answered Betty's questions about make-up. Rev. Geren sat there with a sly smile on his face. He knew me so well he could almost read my mind.

At about 11 p.m. it was time to take Betty home. At that time I had a Fiat car with the engine in the rear. It was small, and two people in the front seat had to sit close. I'm going to like this, I thought.

When we arrived at her apartment building, I asked if I could come the next night and pick her up before the service. She said that wasn't necessary. The fellow she had been coming with could bring her, and I could bring her home after the service. "After all," she said, "you will be preaching, and you need to be ready."

"Don't you think that fellow will be upset if I bring you home?"

"Oh, no. We're just friends who enjoy going to operas together," she said. I doubted that the fellow felt that way.

Sure enough, the next night they showed up for the service. When I got a chance I asked her, "Did you tell him I am taking you home?"

"Not yet. I'll tell him after the service." I was feeling great!

After the service she casually mentioned to him that I was taking her out to eat and that I would be driving her home. He really got angry. He got in his car and peeled rubber taking off from the parking lot.

"What's the matter with him?" she wondered.

"Someday I'll tell you about it," I said. I knew just how he felt. I also knew somehow that she was the girl the Lord had for me.

When we arrived at her house, I said, "I had better come for you tomorrow night."

"You don't have to do that. He'll bring me." I knew he wasn't about to return, and I was afraid she would not be in the service.

Sure enough, the next night she didn't show up. I was sick at heart. I determined that I was going to find her and bring her to church the next night. The problem was I didn't know where she worked or where her apartment was in the large building.

The next afternoon I drove to Trenton and parked my car on Perry Street in front of her apartment building. I started knocking on doors asking where the Barney's lived. Finally I found a lady who knew the Barneys, and she gave me their apartment number. "I saw Betty's mother leave a little while ago," the lady said. I knocked at their apartment, and sure enough no one was home. I sat down on the apartment steps and asked every lady I saw if she was Betty's mother. After about an hour I saw a lady approaching who was as short as Betty, who was only five feet tall.

"Are you Mrs. Barney?" I asked.

"Yes," she said.

I introduced myself. "I'm Bill Maher. I'm the one who is preaching at Shadyrest, and I have been bringing Betty home after the service. Please tell her I will pick her up at 6 p.m." I didn't wait for a reply.

When I arrived at the apartment at 6 p.m., Betty was waiting for me. She looked beautiful. I got out of the car to open the door for her.

"I'm glad you came for me. My friend refused to take me back to Shadyrest. In fact, he won't even speak to me," she said.

That's great! I thought. Then out loud I said, "That's too bad."

What a hypocrite I was.

After the service we got something to eat, and I took her home about midnight. "I'll come for you the same time tomorrow night," I told her. "By the way, it will be my last night. I'll be holding meetings in other churches, and I won't get home to Florida until the middle of October."

"Well, we'll just make the best of it," she said.

I picked Betty up again at six the next evening. There was something I needed to talk to her about after the service. As usual, she waited for me while I talked to people leaving. Then I said good-bye to everyone, for I was leaving early the next morning to hold meetings in Conneautville, Pennsylvania. As we got in my car, I told the Gerens we would be back late, so they shouldn't wait up for me. We headed off for some place to eat, and I was praying about the question I wanted to ask Betty.

We had burgers and coffee. Then we decided we would go for a ride before going home. I was very nervous. I screwed up my courage and blurted, "There is something on my mind. I need to ask you something."

"What is that, Bill?" she asked innocently.

My heart was pounding. "Um," I gulped. "Will you be my wife? I know we've only had three dates before tonight, but I know the Lord wants you and me to be husband and wife. Betty, I love you very much." I finally got it all out. I held my breath waiting for her answer.

"Are you sure? Have you prayed about it?" She still had that innocent expression on her face. *Just say yes!*

"Of course I have. Why do you think I am asking you to be my wife? Now you have to answer 'yes' or 'no.' I do hope you say 'yes.' " I was a nervous wreck, but I think she was enjoying playing me along.

"But Bill, what would people say if we were to get married after only four dates? We haven't had time to get to know each other."

"Who cares?" I cried. "If God wants us together, then why waste time waiting? This is just between us, besides, we could be spending our money to set up our own home."

She gave me a big smile. "You're right, Bill. My answer is 'yes!' I'll marry you as soon as possible!" I began to breathe again. I was the happiest fellow on earth. God was giving me everything I had ever dreamed of.

We talked about when the wedding should take place. "I'll be home about the middle of October," I reminded her. "You could fly down the first week of November."

"That sounds good. I could quit my job at the end of October," she added. "What airport should I fly to?"

"How about Jacksonville?" I said. "It isn't far from where I'm staying. Then we can look for a place to set up our home." I looked at her. I wished we could get married right away, but I knew that wasn't possible.

"How about the end of November?" I asked her. "This will give us time to make the announcement, and you can meet my parents." We settled on November 30, 1957.

"What will your parents think, Bill? Do you think they will like me?"

"Who cares? I'm the one you are marrying. But I'm sure they will love you."

We talked on into the night, dreaming and making plans.

I was so happy I couldn't sleep. In a few hours I headed out on the road. I was eager to finish my meetings and get back to Florida. November couldn't come too soon for me.

After my meetings in Pennsylvania and Youngstown, Ohio, I arrived back in Lorain. I stayed with my sister and her husband, Bill and Lenore Eastin, for my parents had moved to Bradenton, Florida, in September. My happiness at the prospect of my upcoming wedding must have been evident, for Lenore finally asked me, "Bill, what's wrong with you? You act like you're in love. Hey! You're blushing! You do have a girlfriend! Now you sit down here and tell me all about her."

Tell her I did. We had a long talk about my favorite subject, Betty Barney. Then I told her we were going to be married.

"Bill, do Mom and Dad know about this?" asked Lenore.

"Not yet. They'll find out when I take Betty to meet them."

After having meetings in the area, I headed south. It was

already the third week in October. When I got as far as Alabama, my Fiat broke down. I found a motel with a restaurant, and from there I called a mechanic. Fiats were not well known in that area. They would have to send for parts.

I stayed at the motel for four days, praying that I would have enough money to pay for the motel, the food, and the car repairs. I wrote to Betty telling her of my misfortune. Finally my car was fixed, and I left on a Friday and arrived in Ocala on Sunday. I was broke. Many letters were waiting for me, but I was looking for a special one from the girl I was going to marry. There it was! I tore it open and read when to meet her at the Jacksonville airport. She had also sent me a check to help with my expenses.

WEDDING PREPARATIONS

Time was getting short, and I was getting excited. I had to get everything ready for my wife. The Stiples consented to let Betty stay with them for a few days until I could find an apartment for us. Betty would move in immediately and I would join her there after the wedding. I found a one-bedroom apartment on the second floor of a big, old house next to the Jewish synagogue. The assistant pastor of the Central Baptist Church lived on the first floor.

The Saturday finally arrived when Betty would catch a flight in Philadelphia and fly to Jacksonville. I borrowed a friend's car to pick her up. I wanted to be sure to make it there and back. I got there plenty early so I could find where to meet her.

Her plane arrived, and there she was! After hugs and kisses, I gathered her luggage and we headed for Ocala. I admit I took the long way home along the back roads to Berachah Colony. I didn't know it at the time, but Betty didn't like Florida. It was hot compared to New Jersey, and she thought the Spanish moss hanging from the trees was spooky!

The next day I presented Betty to the people of Central Baptist Church. After the service we asked Rev. Walter Faust to perform the ceremony on November 30, and he said he would.

We got our blood tests and marriage license. The next thing I had to do was introduce Betty to my parents. I called Mom to let her know I was bringing over someone very special to meet them. The next Saturday I picked up Betty. She looked beautiful in her yellow dress. Wow, in just a week this beautiful girl would be my wife. I again praised the Lord for His goodness. All the way to my parents' house, Betty kept asking if I thought my parents would like her. I kept assuring her they would.

It was almost noon when we arrived. I got out and opened Betty's door for her. We walked to the door and knocked. Mom opened the door. She looked surprised, then a big smile spread across her face. Dad walked up and I introduced them to Betty. Dad had eyes only for Betty. He took her in and left me standing there at the door. I'm glad Mom let me come in.

After we ate dinner, Betty helped Mom in the kitchen. When they were finished she came out in the living room and sat down next to me on the couch. "Why don't you tell them now?" she whispered. "I want to see how they'll react."

"Mom and Dad," I said, "I have an announcement to make. Betty and I are going to be married."

They didn't act surprised. "When will this take place?" Mom asked.

"Are you ready for this?" I asked.

"Yes," Dad said.

"Next week, on November 30, in the afternoon."

"When?" they both said, not sure if they heard right.

"Next Saturday afternoon at the Central Baptist Church. Rev. Walter Faust will perform the ceremony. There will be a reception afterward. I hope you will be there," I said, knowing they wouldn't miss it.

"We'll be there for sure," Dad said. My parents, and especially Dad, were pleased with Betty and welcomed her to the family. They spent the next week inviting their friends to the wedding.

A WEDDING TO REMEMBER

The big day finally arrived. The weather was a little cool, but I thought it was a perfect day for a wedding. I was eager to get this thing over with.

Betty paid for the whole wedding and reception, her wedding dress, and even our one-night honeymoon at Daytona Beach. Betty Cordrey played the piano, Andy Stiples was best man, and his wife Betty was matron of honor. Dr. D. E. Luttrell gave away the bride. Everything went along just fine until Betty was to put the ring on my finger. For some reason we dropped the ring and it rolled across the floor. Instead of just leaving it there and pronouncing us man and wife, Rev. Faust and Betty Stiples raced to retrieve the ring from under the grand piano. Rev. Faust won. "Try it again," he said.

"Hand it here," I told him, and I slipped the ring on my finger myself.

It finally ended. Pictures were taken, we had cake and punch at the reception, then sneaked away to our apartment to change clothes. As we were leaving for our honeymoon, the mailman came by with a package from friends in Ohio. I told Betty to sign for it while I loaded our luggage in the car.

When I returned she was still standing there. "What's the matter?" I asked.

"A couple of hours ago my name was Barney. What is it now?" You can imagine what the mailman was thinking.

"It's Maher," I said.

"Oh, that's right," she said, and began to sign for the package. Then she hesitated. "How do you spell it?"

"You've got to be kidding! It's M-A-H-E-R!"

"Oh yes," she said, and signed her new name for the first time.

8

THE NEWLYWEDS

As we drove toward Daytona Beach, we noticed the weather was changing and getting much cooler, but we didn't care. We were happy to be married and on our honeymoon.

We checked in at our motel about 6 p.m., then headed to the S & S Cafeteria to eat. We were both beaming with happiness. Our waitress asked if we had just gotten married. With crimson faces, we admitted that we had just that afternoon.

We went back to the motel, and we noticed that our room was really cool.

"Turn on the heat," Betty said, and I did. But it was still cold. We put all the blankets on the bed that we could find, but by the next morning we were freezing. The temperature was in the twenties.

We packed up and left early. After breakfast we went to St. Augustine for the day. We arrived back at our apartment after dark. Several more packages were waiting for us at the door. We carried them inside our very cold apartment, which had only one small gas heater. There was also a fireplace in the bedroom, so we hurriedly built a fire with the boxes and wrapping paper from our packages.

"There is something I forgot to tell you, Bill. Please don't talk to me in the morning until after I've had my coffee," warned Betty.

"Oh, come on," I said. "You've got to be kidding." I didn't believe her.

"No, I'm not, Bill. I'm not civilized until I've had my coffee."

The first thing the next morning I gave her a hug and cheerfully said, "Good morning!" All I got in return was a sneer. Once she had her coffee she was fine. I couldn't believe that a cup of coffee could make such a difference.

That night before we went to bed, I set the percolator and a cup on her side of the bed. The next morning I got up and started the coffee. Soon the noise from the percolator woke Betty.

"What's that?" said Betty.

"It's coffee brewing," I said. "I want you to drink some before you get out of bed!" We both laughed, and she had her coffee. She is still the same after all the years we have been married.

At this time I was getting only forty dollars a month, which paid for the rent. If anything else came in, we paid bills first before buying food. We found we weren't eating much, and at times the aroma of cooking coming from the first floor made our mouths water. Sometimes we would go for a walk during meal time to avoid the delicious smells.

We walked a lot to save money on gas. We had no TV or radio, and our big entertainment on Saturday was watching people walk by on their way to the synagogue next door.

SPEAKING AT A CHRISTIAN UNIVERSITY

I continued to travel, preaching in different churches. One place where I got regular invitations to preach was at the Tabernacle Baptist Church in Wilson, North Carolina, where Rev. Otis Holmes was the pastor. After being with Rev. Holmes five times, he asked me if I had ever been to Bob Jones University.

"No, I haven't," I replied.

He seemed to think this was strange. "Well, why not?"

I thought I would have some fun with him. "I've never been there for one good reason!" I said emphatically.

"And what is that?" he demanded, thinking I had something against the place.

With a smirk I said, "Because they have never invited me."

Being a good sport, Rev. Holmes laughed and asked, "When can you be there?" I checked my calendar and found I had an open week in April.

"I'll be in Spartanburg, South Carolina, on a Sunday, and I could drive over to Greenville on Monday," I told him.

"Then consider yourself booked. You be there on Monday,"

he said.

"Oh sure, I am going to walk on campus and they will welcome me with open arms," I said sarcastically. "I doubt they have ever heard of me."

"You sure are hard to please," Rev. Holmes said. "Okay, this is what I'll do. I will have Dr. Jones send you a letter requesting you be there on this date."

"If you can do that," I promised, "I'll be there." I didn't think there was any possibility that I would get a letter from Dr. Jones at the great Christian university. I didn't exactly think I was famous.

I mentioned this incident to Betty after I returned home. We both thought it was strange that Rev. Holmes could be so sure that he could get me an invitation to speak at Bob Jones University. About a week later Betty returned from the post office all excited. There was a letter from Bob Jones University. I quickly opened the envelope. Inside was a letter from Dr. Gilbert Stenholm, the director of the ministerial training, asking me to speak to the "preacher boys" and in chapel. I was told to be there the morning after I spoke in Spartanburg. There was some shouting at the Maher house. Betty and I were thrilled and amazed that God would open this door. I could hardly wait until April of 1958 arrived.

April arrived at last. I preached at the Church of the Open Door in Spartanburg and spent the night with the pastor and his family. I decided to get up early to drive over to Greenville. It was only about 35 miles, but I wanted a little time to look the place over before it was time for me to speak. Somehow I assumed that it was a small place, so I was in for a surprise when I arrived. I drove through the entrance on my way to the administration building, amazed at the large and beautiful campus. I wondered what I had gotten myself into, or rather what Rev. Holmes had gotten me into.

When I approached the door of the administration building, I saw a man there at the door. He asked a group of people ahead of me if any of them was Rev. William Maher. "I'm William Maher," I called out, thinking there must have been some message for me.

The man was obviously upset. "I'm Gilbert Stenholm. Where have you been? You're supposed to be teaching a class right now, and you have four other classes to teach." *What? I had never taught college classes!* "Didn't you get my letter?" Dr. Stenholm went on. "I told you the first class started at 8 a.m.!" He glanced at his watch. "You still have about 45 minutes left in the class."

"Wait a minute! What class am I teaching?" I asked. "And what letter was I supposed to have received? I didn't get a letter about teaching. The only letter I got from you mentioned speaking in the preacher boys class and chapel."

"Hold it right here," Dr. Stenholm said. He charged up the stairs to his office. Soon he came slowly back down the stairs holding in his hands the letter that was supposed to have been sent to me a couple of weeks ago. "Brother Maher, I owe you an apology. Somehow this letter never got mailed to you. I am very sorry I was upset with you. Please forgive me." He was embarrassed and sincerely sorry, and I assured him I was not offended. I was impressed that this doctor could be so humble.

That day I taught in five classes along with speaking to the preacher boys and in chapel to all the students and faculty. By the end of the day I was exhausted, but happy. Who would have ever believed that a handicapped preacher could have an opportunity like this?

That evening Dr. Stenholm wanted to do something special for me, so he had a special showing of a new film called *Red Runs the River.* The film was produced by Bob Jones University under the direction of his wife, Dr. Katherine Stenholm. He even supplied popcorn and Coca-Cola. By now I was glad he had made the mistake. We soon became fast friends.

Although I had never taught a class in a college, institute, or university, I must have done an adequate job, for I have had the privilege to do so at BJU and other institutions since that time. In fact, some of the current BJU professors remember when they were students in classes I taught. One is Dr. Thurman Wisdom, who is now the dean of the School of Religion.

As I left Bob Jones University on my way to preach in

Missouri, I was rejoicing and praising the Lord for the privilege I had to teach and preach there. One thing still puzzled me though. How did Otis Holmes arrange this?

When I arrived in Missouri, I bragged to the pastor about preaching at Bob Jones University. I told him I still didn't understand how Rev. Holmes had arranged it.

This pastor knew Rev. Holmes and began to laugh. "You mean to tell me that you preach for Brother Holmes and he never told you his connection with Bob Jones University?"

"No," I replied. "All I know about him is that he is pastor of Tabernacle Baptist Church in Wilson, North Carolina."

When the pastor could stop laughing, he said, "Brother Holmes is the brother-in-law of Dr. Bob Jones Jr. and serves on the Executive Committee of the university. Dr. Jones married Brother Holmes' sister."

I laughed too. No wonder he could say with such confidence, "Be sure to be there on Monday."

Later I wrote to Brother Holmes and asked why he hadn't told me about his connection with Bob Jones University. I liked his reply: "I do not want to be known as the brother-in-law of Dr. Bob Jones Jr., not that I am ashamed of this. I would rather be known as one who loves the Lord Jesus Christ and is faithfully serving him." We became good friends, and I became "Uncle Bill" to his daughters. My admiration for this man and his wife has grown over the years.

LEARNING TO LIVE BY FAITH

Earlier in that year of 1958, Betty had announced to me that she was going to get a job. "We've got to have more money," she told me. "You need to keep preaching and working with the afflicted." While she looked for a job, I visited people with all kinds of handicaps in Marion County. I would talk to their families, too, about their need for the Savior.

Betty soon found a job at a place that made orange crates. It didn't last long because the business closed. Then she found a job decorating cakes. The employer really took advantage of the women who worked there, for they worked hard with little pay. Betty made less than half what she had received in New Jersey. She soon quit this job in frustration over the working conditions for women.

"Okay, Bill, I'm not going to work anymore," she said. "I will stay home and be a full-time wife. You said the Lord will supply our every need. Now you will be the one to bring home the bacon."

"Fine," I said. I couldn't blame her, but I confess I was kind of nervous about what was going to happen now. She had more faith than I did that the Lord would meet our needs. What an encouragement she was to me.

Then when I least expected it, she dropped a bomb. "We are going to get a washing machine," she announced. "I'm tired of spending our money going to get our clothes washed. We could take that money and use it to make monthly payments on a washing machine of our own." Betty and I had been living independently for a long time before we were married, and we both were set in our ways. The way she made her announcement, I knew I dared not open my mouth to object.

"Can I ask a question?"

"Yes," she said.

"What are we going to use for a down payment?"

"I have fifty dollars from my Christmas club savings," she said. "We will use that. You said that the Lord will take care of us, so let's believe it. Now it's time to practice what you've been preaching." My wife, who had been saved only a short time, put me to shame with her faith. I'm glad she was on my side.

We went to Marion County Hardware Store, just a few blocks from our apartment. They carried the Frigidaire brand that Betty wanted. We looked at the various models trying to find the least expensive one.

Soon the manager walked over and asked if he could be of any help. Betty told him we needed a washer.

"Which one did you like?" he asked.

"Which one is the cheapest?" we wanted to know. He showed us, and we made our selection.

"Are you going to pay cash or put it on credit?" asked the manager.

"Credit," we said in unison.

"How much will you put down?"

"Fifty dollars," Betty answered.

"Do you want to make payments monthly or weekly?" asked the man.

"Monthly," Betty said.

"That's fine. Now since we don't know you, we need to know how much money you make a week."

"I don't know," I replied.

"Well how much do you make in a month or year?"

Oh boy, how was I going to explain? "I'm sorry sir, I don't know that either. You see, I am in the ministry doing evangelistic work with the handicapped. We walk by faith, and the Lord always meets our needs." I sounded a lot more confident than I felt right then.

"I've heard about people like you, but you're the first I've met. You say God will supply all your need?" he asked.

"That's right, sir," I said rather halfheartedly. This crafty salesman was setting me up.

"I'll tell you what," he said. "You get the best washer we have and I will knock fifty dollars off the price. Prove to me that your God can take care of the payments," he dared us.

I was about to say we would go home and talk about it when Betty said confidently, "That's fine with me. You can deliver it this afternoon." I was about to pass out.

The washer was delivered that afternoon, and we prayed. My wife really knew how to talk to the Lord.

At the end of six months we went to make the last payment. "That's the first time I have ever seen faith in action," the store manager said. "You can have credit on anything else in the store." He was open to our witness now, but to our knowledge he never received Christ. Perhaps we planted a seed that someone else could reap. Anyway, this was the beginning of many steps Betty and I took by faith.

I was about to leave to hold meetings in the north when Betty announced that next step. "Bill, you need to get a new suit."

"What's wrong with the ones I have?" I wanted to know.

"They are cheap, and once you wear them they look like you have slept in them. You are an ambassador for the Lord, and you should look like one," she explained.

"Before we were married I thought you were satisfied with the way I looked," I said.

"I was and still am," she assured me, "but shouldn't we look our best for Christ?"

I gave up. "Okay, where are we going?" I asked, thinking it would be something like J. C. Penney or Sears.

"I'm thinking of Kennedy's Men's Clothing Store," she announced.

I protested. "But they sell the most expensive suits in town."

"That's right," she agreed, then added, "and they are worth the price." So away we went down town to Kennedy's.

"These suits look good," she said as we looked over a rack of suits in my size, and I had to agree. Betty enjoyed picking out several suits for me to try on.

"May I help you?" a salesman asked.

"My husband is interested in one of these suits," Betty said before I could open my mouth. The man measured me, then made sure I had the right size and showed me where to change.

When I came out of the dressing room in the one Betty liked the best, she told the salesman, "We'll take this one." I looked at the price tag on the sleeve and saw $125! I almost fainted.

"Betty!" I whispered. "I could buy four suits for the price of this one!"

"That's the whole problem, Bill, and you would look terrible. Please get this one. Do it for me." My resistance was crumbling, but I made one last stand.

"But how are we going to pay for this?"

"The same way we paid for the washer," she assured me. She said "we," but I knew it was her faith that brought in the money.

We told the salesman we wanted to buy the suit and how we wanted to pay for it. "You will have to talk to Mr. Kennedy about your credit," he said. I was actually relieved, for I was sure Mr.

Kennedy would not allow us to buy anything on credit.

The salesman called for Mr. Kennedy. "Can I help you?" he asked.

I told Mr. Kennedy my name was Rev. Bill Maher and I wanted to buy a suit on credit.

"Did you say your name is Rev. Bill Maher?" asked Mr. Kennedy. "Are you the one who bought the washer from Marion County Hardware?"

"Yes sir."

"Then you can buy anything you want." He gave the salesman permission to have the suit altered.

The light went on in Betty's head. "We'll take two suits, and two or three shirts and ties." And Betty prayed them off in no time.

A VISIT TO NEW JERSEY

When we were first married, Betty did not like Florida, especially Ocala. She wished she could go back to New Jersey. So she was very pleased when I told her we were going to be in New Jersey from June until September. She would get to see her mother, and I would get to know my mother-in-law.

We saved what little money we could to cover our expenses during the two days it would take us to get there. We were to take care of Shadyrest Bible Conference while the Gerens took a well-deserved two-week vacation. After they returned we would continue to help with the work.

"Work" was an understatement, as Betty soon learned. She helped clean the big mansion, cooked and served meals, and did whatever else needed to be done. She did manage to find a little time to visit her mother and her sister Lois. I painted, mowed the grass, and fixed whatever needed repair. I also managed to do some preaching.

Betty's mother worked at a restaurant. I had met her briefly only one time at the apartment she and Betty used to share. One day Betty and I decided to eat at the restaurant where Betty's mother worked. It was the first time I would really be introduced, and I was a bit nervous. During the formal introductions, I noticed again how short and thin Betty's mother was. When Betty's mom took our order of hot dogs and fries, I noticed that she kept staring at me.

"Why did your mother keep looking at me so funny?" I asked Betty.

"I don't know, but I noticed it too. I'll just go ask her." Soon Betty returned laughing.

"What's so funny?" I wanted to know.

"Since she really didn't remember you, Mother thought I married the blond fellow who was taking me to Shadyrest when we met. She was wondering where you came from!" I smiled at her anyway, hoping she wasn't too disappointed and that she would like me.

After about a month into the summer Betty wanted to go home. For some reason Florida began to look good to her.

"Sorry, kid. We promised to help out, and we still have the trip to visit all the churches before we go home," I reminded her. She never complained again, although plenty happened on our trip that she could have complained about. For instance, after a long, tiring journey it was common for us to be greeted at someone's house like this: "Come in! Brother Maher, you rest yourself in this chair, or lie down in the bedroom if you'd like. Sister Maher, you can help me in the kitchen." Betty was as tired as I was, but people would assume that since she wasn't doing the driving that she wasn't tired. Betty never complained, but I could tell it was hard for her.

We finally arrived at my sister's house in Ohio. The Eastin family was very eager to meet Betty. We enjoyed our stay there while speaking in different Baptist churches in the area.

LEARNING THE TRUTH OF ROMANS 8:28

One Baptist church in particular was an example of what I often faced in those days. We had weekend meetings there with some very positive results. After the Sunday evening service we were given an envelope. We went out to the car before we opened it. To our surprise, it contained a check for only twenty-five dollars.

"How are we going to get home on just twenty-five dollars?" Betty asked.

"I don't know," I replied. "Maybe we can borrow some money from the Eastins." I sure didn't want to though, for with their four children I knew they didn't have much extra money. While still sitting in the car, we prayed that the Lord would provide a better way to get us home. About that time one of the deacons spotted us and walked over to the car.

"Wow, I'm sure glad you folks got a good offering tonight!" he exclaimed. I didn't know what to say. I just showed him the check. He looked shocked when he saw it.

"How can this be? I gave one hundred dollars myself!" he exclaimed. "Let me have that check," he said. He grabbed the check out of my hand and stormed into the building with it. He was very upset.

"What's he going to do?" wondered Betty.

"I don't know, but it should be pretty interesting." It was cold outside, so we went in and sat down in the auditorium to wait.

Soon we heard the deacon yelling, "You're a thief! Brother Maher received more than twenty-five dollars in his offering. I put in a hundred dollars myself, and I know others who put in that much or more. Where is it?"

The pastor tried to placate the deacon. "Brother Maher doesn't need as much as we do because he is afflicted. I told the treasurer to pay some of the church's bills and make out a check to cover my salary. That will save the church some money."

"We'll see about that!" the angry deacon snapped. He called some other deacons to return to the church. When they arrived he said, "We have two thieves in this church," and he told them what happened. Then everything broke loose!

In a few minutes the deacons came into the auditorium where we sat. The same deacon acted as their spokesman. "Brother and Sister Maher, we are sorry about all of this. We want to make up for this somehow," he said nervously. "We can give you $350 for now, but there was much more in your offering. I'm afraid some of the money is already spent. Please forgive us," he pleaded, and told us what had taken place. Of course, we had heard most of it already. He was embarrassed and ashamed of his pastor's actions. I really felt sorry for him.

"If you don't mind, this is what we'll do: We will start supporting you for twenty-five dollars a month until we have paid you everything you have coming. Then we will continue to support you until the Lord takes us all home. How will that be?"

We were thrilled, and I answered, "It would be wonderful if you did this." We left with $350 in our pocket and twenty-five dollars a month support. We heard later that the church treasurer was fired, and the pastor left shortly thereafter. Nearly forty years later, they still support us, but for a far greater amount. Don't tell me that Romans 8:28 isn't true.

MINISTERING IN FLORIDA

Finally it was time to head home. Betty was a bit sick, but I just attributed it to her being tired after all the travel. Unlike me, she never was much of a complainer, and I didn't pay much attention to her sickness.

It took us two days to drive home. We arrived about the second week of November. Remembering how Betty had not liked Florida, and especially Ocala, I couldn't believe how glad she was to see our little apartment in the old house. "I can be in my own bed," she rejoiced. "I don't want to leave again." She was her old self. Even though it was an old apartment, it was home to us.

We spent Thanksgiving with my parents, and right after the holiday I asked Dr. Earl McQuay, pastor of Grace Baptist Church in Sarasota, if I could preach for him. He gave me permission to come right away. At that time the church was small, but they took us on as one of their supported missionaries. Again we rejoiced. It was the beginning of many churches in that area taking us on for support. At this time I was asked to help them, along with Calvary Baptist in Bradenton, to start a work among the afflicted.

A building that had once been a motel had been converted

into a housing facility for the afflicted. It was located about half-way between Sarasota and Bradenton, and this is where I would begin right after the new year in 1959.

In January we drove to the housing facility for the afflicted and began visiting them. We asked them to go to church at Grace Baptist if they were from Sarasota, or to Calvary Baptist if they were from Bradenton. We preached in these churches as well, asking Christians to treat the afflicted with the same kindness that Christ would show. Many of these afflicted people trusted Christ as their Savior.

As you may guess, the devil didn't like what we were doing, but God kept us doing his work. We were still driving the Fiat, and now it tried to fall apart. The headliner, the inner cloth of the roof, came loose and fell down on the seats. We propped it up with a broom. Then the muffler fell off as we drove down the road. That made us the center of attention for a while. The motor started acting up, but a friend took charge of the car and returned it to us in good shape. He even filled the tank with gas so we could continue to reach the afflicted for Christ.

The Lord used many people to take care of us. Folks often invited us over for meals, and we had great times of fellowship. We continued to travel regularly to Sarasota and Bradenton to work with the handicapped.

THE MAHERS BECOME PARENTS

Betty was not feeling well again, so she asked Betty Cordrey if she could recommend a doctor. She recommended Dr. Webb, a Christian man who specialized in caring for women. We made an appointment.

Betty and I went to see Dr. Webb, and I took an immediate liking to him. He said he and his wife had eleven children. Then I sat in the waiting room while Betty had some tests.

Soon Betty came out with a smirk on her face. "Well, what did the doctor say?" I asked. No answer, just a smile.

All the way home I asked Betty what was wrong, but she kept silent. When we got home, I pleaded, "Come on, what did he say is wrong with you?"

"Do you really want to know?" she teased.

"Don't do this to me, Betty. Yes, I really want to know!"

"Are you really ready for this?"

"Okay!" I shouted. "Enough of this! Stop teasing me and tell what Dr. Webb said is wrong with you!"

"All right," my dear wife calmly said. "You are going to become a father. My due date is June 2."

"Huh? Tell me again, I don't think I heard right. Say that to me again, slowly."

Laughing, she said, "Bill, you are going to be a father and I will be a mother. That does happen, you know."

Slowly it dawned on me what she had said. I was beside myself with joy. "You're not kidding me, are you? We are really going to be parents?"

"Yep," she replied. I grabbed her in a bear hug.

We made the usual phone calls to family and friends to announce the good news. Over the next few months we enjoyed all of the events typical of expectant parents-regular visits to the doctor, baby showers, picking out names. We settled on William Thomas Maher if we had a boy. If the baby was a girl, we decided on Elizabeth Margaret Maher. The people at Graham Road Baptist Church gave us a new crib and some baby blankets, and a family in the church gave us money to help pay the medical bills. The Lord was gracious in providing all of these things for us.

One thing happened that I wasn't prepared for. I had heard about how pregnant women sometimes had cravings for food at strange times, but I didn't think about this happening to Betty. Then Betty woke me one night by sweetly saying, "Do you love me, Bill?"

"Huh? Why are you asking such a silly question?"

"Do you really love me?" Betty asked softly and sweetly.

I sat up and looked at the clock. Three a.m.! Now I was wondering what she was up to. "All right. By now you know that I love you. What's this all about?" I asked.

"I'm hungry, Bill. I really would like a steak sandwich. You said you really love me. Will you get the woman you love a steak sandwich?"

"A steak sandwich? Where am I going to get a steak sandwich at three in the morning?"

Betty didn't get excited at my objections. "You said you love me, that you really love me," she said in that same sweet voice. "I want a steak sandwich."

I gave up. I dressed and set out to find a restaurant that would make a steak sandwich at three a.m. Besides, I was thinking, If I find a place, I'll get one for me too. She's not the only one who likes steak sandwiches!

After driving around town for a while I found a place that was open. It was very quiet when I walked in. One of the ladies working there knew me and asked, "What are you doing out at this time of the morning?"

"My wife wants a steak sandwich. I hope you have them. If you do I'll take one too."

The waitress looked at me slyly. "Before I tell you if we have steak sandwiches, I want you to answer a question for me: Is your wife expecting a baby?" I nodded in the affirmative. "I thought so!" she exclaimed, and the other workers cheered. "We do have steak sandwiches."

I took the sandwiches home to my sweet wife. "Please don't do this again," I requested.

"You didn't have to get yourself one," she reminded me. "I'm the one who is having a baby, not you; but I am thankful to have a husband who loves me enough to get me what I crave."

I couldn't argue with this woman. She always seemed to be one step ahead of me. But that was the only time she ever asked me to satisfy a craving. She may have had others, but if she did she didn't mention them to me. She probably wanted to save money for when the baby arrived.

While waiting for the baby to come, we continued to be involved in ministering to the afflicted. We had a list of names of the afflicted in our county, and we visited them. We also visited many in Sarasota and Bradenton. We became close to many of these people and their families.

Once I received a call to go to the hospital to see a young

man we had gotten to know named R. John. He was afflicted with muscular dystrophy. R. John could not walk, and he had no use of his hands except for two fingers. His speaking ability was very limited. And now R. John had been severely burned. Little did I know what I was about to face.

I rushed into the emergency room. The family doctor met me and asked if I was the preacher R. John's parents had called. I told him I was. The doctor told me that the parents had already arrived. When the parents had seen R. John, his mother had fainted and his father had had a heart attack. They were both being treated, the doctor explained. Then he brought me into the room to see R. John.

I could understand why R. John's parents had reacted the way they did. He was lying on a hard table, covered with blisters from the top of his head to the soles of his feet. He looked up at me, his eyes pleading. I felt the tears roll down my face, for I was helpless to do anything for him. But I knew Who could, and I prayed with him. While the medical personnel worked on R. John's injuries, the doctor asked me to stay with him until they could move him to a special room. Soon his mother appeared, but his father was still receiving medical attention.

I continued to visit R. John during his hospitalization. One time I took another preacher with me, but he left in a hurry. He couldn't stand the sight of R. John's terrible burns. Another time when Rev. Geren was holding meetings at a nearby church, I took him to see R. John. As he looked at R. John, Rev. Geren said, "That's what hell is like—continual pain in a lake of fire." *How true that is,* I thought. R. John lived two years in constant pain before the Lord took him home.

About this time I met a group of parents who were interested in starting a school that could meet the needs of their children with Down's Syndrome. They looked to me for guidance. We spent a lot of time talking about the arrangements necessary for such a school. Then I scheduled a meeting at the county health department on June 2. I reminded the parents to be there at 1 p.m. I had a vague recollection that June 2 was Betty's due date, but babies are never born on the exact day the doctors said they will be. Are they?

On June 2 Betty woke me at 6 a.m. with the news, "Our baby will be born today."

Like the typical first-time father, I did what was normal. I panicked. I bolted out of bed and raced around the room.

"Why are you getting up?" Betty inquired.

"You said the baby is going to be born today," I replied, dressing as fast as I could.

Betty laughed. "I've never seen you move so fast. Don't worry, dear, it will be a while yet. I was just reminding you that we are going to be parents before this day is over."

"How can you know this?" I demanded. My sweet wife just smiled.

Betty got breakfast, then started cleaning the apartment. She even got down on her hands and knees.

"Why are you cleaning now?" I asked.

She looked at me as though I had just asked a dumb question. "Your parents are going to be here, and I want the place to look nice," she informed me.

"Who cares? You are having a baby! Don't overdo it," I pleaded. "Why don't you just forget the cleaning?" I was a nervous wreck.

"Bill, don't you have a meeting today with those mothers who want to start a school? Shouldn't you be getting ready for it?" she reminded me. In my excitement I had forgotten all about it.

"Oh, yes. I had better postpone it," I said.

"Please don't. The baby will not be born until tonight. Why don't you call Dr. Webb, if it will put your mind at ease. I'm sure he will agree with me." How could she know all of this?

I called Dr. Webb about the problem I was having with Betty. He chuckled and reassured me that Mother knows best. "Besides, if you check in the hospital after 2 p.m. you'll save money." He knew how to appeal to me. "If you check in earlier you'll be charged for today, and that would be wasted." I agreed to try to wait until after 2 p.m.

The special meeting at the health department began at

1 p.m. as scheduled. Several mothers were there, and even some fathers who were able to take off work. Every time I heard a phone ring somewhere in the building, I thought it would be Betty calling me to take her to the hospital. I nervously watched the clock as time slowly ticked by. Somehow we made progress in the meeting in spite of my lack of attention. The decision was made to begin a school that fall near the old airport, off Route 200. The meeting ended about 3 p.m.

I raced back home expecting to find Betty standing with her bags in her hand, ready to depart for the hospital. Instead there she sat, quietly reading and resting. How could she be calm at a time like this? "Aren't you ready to go?" I asked incredulously.

"I guess I am. But Bill, you're a mess! Everything is fine, really. I'm doing great," she reassured me.

We got together her things and got in the car. "Why don't you stop and get a newspaper to read? It's still going to be a while before the baby will be born," she said.

"You're kidding!"

"No, I'm not. It will be boring waiting. You need something to help the time pass." She was right about that! I stopped on the way to the hospital and picked up a copy of the evening paper, the *Ocala Star Banner.*

We finally arrived at the hospital about 4:30 p.m. Dr. Webb was there to greet us, and Betty was taken to the delivery room. I laid the paper across her stomach and read while counting the minutes between labor pains. When Betty had a contraction, we would practice a form of arm wrestling. She would take my hand and pull, and I would pull back. I had no idea my sweet tiny wife was so strong. My arm was getting sore by about 9 p.m. when Betty announced, "The baby will be born any minute." I called for Dr. Webb. When he came in I left.

Ten minutes later I was called back in. There was the new mother holding a crying and thrashing black-haired baby. "Bill, I want you to meet Elizabeth Margaret Maher."

I stared in wonder. "She sure can scream," I said. "She has a good pair of lungs. And look at her arms and legs go."

"She's mad at the world," Betty said. "She was comfortable

where she was, but I sure wasn't."

I asked the doctor and nurses to stop what they were doing so we could thank the Lord for taking care of Betty and our new addition. We prayed and gave God the glory for what He had done. Then the nurses took Elizabeth to the nursery and Betty to her room. I headed for the telephone to call our parents. When I returned to Betty's room she was putting up her hair.

"What are you doing?" I cried. "In case you don't remember, you just had a baby. You should be resting instead of fooling with your hair."

"Your mother and father will be here tomorrow and I want to look nice," she said, as though that explained everything. At times, as every man knows, women can be absolutely incomprehensible.

A nurse brought some food in for Betty. I hadn't had anything to eat, and Betty felt sorry for me. "Why don't you go on home. You look tired. Get something to eat, and get some rest." She had just had a baby, and she wasn't as tired as I was. I walked out massaging my sore arm and wondering which was really the weaker sex.

On the way home I found just the right restaurant, a steak place on Pine Street. Mr. Percy Cordrey had often taken us there. When I walked in, the owner said, "Sorry, we are closing for the night." Then he recognized me and asked, "What are you doing here so late?"

"I'm starved!" I exclaimed. "My wife just had a baby girl about an hour and a half ago. I wanted to celebrate with a steak dinner, and now you tell me you're closing."

"Well, congratulations!" the owner said, shaking my hand and grinning. "Put on the grill," he called out to the cook. "We all are going to help Rev. Maher celebrate the birth of his daughter. Cook a steak for each one of us." Then the cook, the owner, and I sat down to a delicious meal of steak, french fries, salad, and coffee. "It's all on the house," the owner said when we were through eating. "I hope you enjoyed it." That I did. I went home full of good food and happy thoughts and dreams for the family the Lord was giving me. I went to bed but I couldn't sleep. It was so strange to be alone in a quiet apartment. That wasn't going to last long.

9

BETH

I arose early in the morning, ate a quick breakfast, and hurried to the hospital. I stopped by the nursery window, but the blinds were closed. I went on to Betty's room. "How's our daughter doing?" I asked as I entered the room.

"Is that all you want to know, how Elizabeth is doing? You don't even ask me how I am doing. Well, Elizabeth is doing fine, and in case you are interested, I'm doing fine too," she remarked. Oh boy, I had done it again. I needed to learn how to talk all over again. Even though we had a child, I needed to remember to put Betty first.

"What are we going to call her?" I asked, hoping to change the subject.

"I've been thinking about that," Betty replied. "How about Beth?"

Beth, I thought to myself. "That sounds great to me. Beth it will be," I proudly pronounced.

It wasn't long before my parents arrived at the hospital. They could hardly wait to see their new granddaughter. They had already checked in at a motel near our apartment. After we visited with Betty for a while, the nurse came in to tell us we could see the baby now. I proudly pointed her out in the nursery. "We are going to call her Beth," I told them. They both liked the name.

The next day we took Betty and Beth home. I quickly learned that two mothers in the same house were a problem. Dad knew how to solve this problem, though; he took Mom home the next day. Now we were left to ourselves to figure out what to do next. I never would have believed how much work was involved in caring for a new baby. There were no disposable diapers in those days, so we washed diapers and baby clothes every day. We enjoyed having Beth with us, but the feedings, diaper changes, burping, and rocking Beth to sleep were very tiring, especially for Betty.

"Let's try something different," she suggested. "Let's take turns feeding the baby. You get up one night, and I'll get up the next night. This way I can at least get some rest every other night."

I thought it was a good idea, so we tried it. It didn't work. I was a sound sleeper and hard of hearing beside, so I never heard Beth's cries in the night. Betty would poke me in the ribs and say, "Beth's crying. It's your turn to feed her." I would get up and give the baby a bottle. Finally Betty decided it was less trouble to just feed Beth herself than to wake me up, for by the time I woke up she was awake anyway.

A NEW HOUSE FOR AN EXPANDING FAMILY

The months went by, and mother and daughter were doing fine. One day in 1960 Betty said, "I had better make an appointment to see Dr. Webb." I assumed she needed to take Beth in for a check-up. I took them to Dr. Webb's office and sat in the waiting room. Soon I was called back to the examining room. Dr. Webb was wearing a grin. "Looks like you are going to be a father again. This time the baby is due on September 12. Take good care of your wife and daughter." I wasn't ready for this. Beth was born June 2, 1959, and now the doctor was telling me we would have another child on September 12, 1960. I had a lot of work to do.

We sent out announcements, and I got busy. We had moved some time before to a farm near Martin, about fifteen miles from Ocala. It was a quiet place, and we liked it even though it wasn't fancy. Betty had worked hard cleaning up the place, and then the owner told us we had to move as soon as possible. We were very upset. Now we had to find another place to live.

I had managed to save $600, and Betty and I began to think about buying a house of our own. That way no one could ever make us move. We bought a tiny two-bedroom, one-bath place on Lynwood Place in Ocala. The house was so small it seemed that we could stand in the middle and touch all four outside walls. There was a small living room and kitchen, a small back porch and an even smaller porch in the front. We were so close to the neighbors' houses that we could hear them snore.

At the end of the street was a cemetery. We joked that if we couldn't live here, we could probably make it at the end of the street! Yet we loved the place, for it was our own.

We had owls and all sorts of wildlife in our neighborhood. Betty even once killed a snake in the kitchen behind the stove.

I took Betty and Beth along when I went to hold meetings at Conneautville Baptist Church up in Pennsylvania. Rev. Howard Little was then the pastor. He and his wife had been married for several years but had no children. They enjoyed Beth so much that Mrs. Little asked Betty and I to pray for her to have a baby. We agreed to pray with them about it. After we got back home Rev. and Mrs. Joe Morone stopped by our house to visit. They too were childless and asked us to pray that they would have a baby. Soon we heard that both couples were going to be parents. "That's it," Betty said. "I'm not praying for anyone else to have a baby until I've had my next one."

My parents came to help us celebrate Beth's first birthday. Beth enjoyed the birthday cake and other goodies along with the gifts. Betty was holding up well as she carried our second child through those hot summer months of 1960. I thanked God that he didn't make men to carry children.

I was to be on the road holding meetings in the middle of September, so I hoped the baby wouldn't be late. On September 9 a hurricane hit Florida, and by the next day, a Sunday, it was very close to Ocala. No one went to church or anywhere else with the big hurricane blowing outside. Betty thought the baby might come a day early, because hurricanes often caused expectant mothers to go into labor. Sure enough, that Sunday afternoon she started having labor pains.

"Do you think we ought to go to the hospital?" she asked me.

"Honey, can't you see those palm trees bending over to the ground? The traffic lights are hanging sideways in that wind. You just can't have the baby today." Like an obedient wife she waited until the hurricane abated the next day before going to the hospital. She was in labor all that day, and on September 12 at 12:53 a.m. we became the proud parents of a son, William

Thomas Maher V. We decided to call him Billy. I was worn out. It was amazing to me how tiring it was to become a father. Betty must have been far more tired than I was, but she sent me on home to rest.

Early the next morning I made the necessary phone calls. My parents had been waiting to hear the good news. They arrived at the hospital that afternoon and Betty was ready to greet them. Dad brought along a baseball and a baseball bat for his newest grandson. He was still a baseball fan.

"Dad, Billy isn't even twenty-four hours old yet. When do you expect him to start playing baseball?"

"As soon as he can walk," replied the proud grandfather.

Beth was excited when we took Billy home. To her he was like a doll that moved. Beth was still a baby herself at fifteen months and had just gotten off the bottle. Now we were a family of four.

Beth noticed how much attention Billy got when he cried, so she tried it. Betty had her hands full taking care of two babies, but she did a great job of it. Just a few days after Billy was born I was back on the road preaching.

AIR TRAVEL

I began having a lot of car trouble while traveling around to preach. My car usually broke down when I was on my way home. I'd call home to tell Betty I would be late, and she would pray for me. I would be very homesick for my family. My eagerness to get home could have been dangerous.

Once after I had finished holding revival meetings at Berlin Baptist Church in Marne, Michigan, I got up early the next morning and headed for home. I should have stopped to rest, but I wanted to get home. I remember crossing the Florida state line and seeing the sign for Marion County. The next thing I knew I woke up in our bed at home. It was morning.

"How did I get here?" I asked Betty.

"That is my question to ask you," said Betty. "I awoke to a car horn in the middle of the night. I went to see what was going on, and there you sat in the driveway leaning on the horn fast asleep. You woke the babies and the whole neighborhood!" she scolded. "I put you to bed. Don't you remember?"

"No, I don't," I confessed. "I drove all the way from Michigan because I missed you and the babies," I said sheepishly.

"Well, we can thank the Lord for His protection." Betty looked at me. "Bill, please do me a favor. Start flying."

"Flying! Do you know how much that costs?" I didn't know what it cost, but I was sure it was expensive. I, who had once liked to throw money around to show off, had become quite a tightwad.

"Just check on it, please?" she said sweetly. "We love you and need you. We can't have you falling asleep at the steering wheel anymore." When she talked to me like that, I couldn't resist. I told her I would check on it, although I thought it was a waste to time.

The next day I called the airlines and asked for prices to fly to certain cities where I frequently traveled. To my surprise, I found that the plane ticket cost about the same as when I traveled by myself and had to pay for gas, food, and motels. Plus I only had to travel one day to reach my destination or return home. This meant more time with my family. Thus the Lord opened up a new method of travel for me.

There was a small airport on Route 200, just a short distance from our house. I bought tickets to travel to my next meeting. I was nervous the first time I boarded one of those propeller-driven planes, but I liked the flight. After this, I frequently flew to places where I had meetings. It was great to leave the driving to the pilots and be able to enjoy the extra time at home without those long tiring trips.

Betty didn't drive a car, so she got her exercise walking to the new shopping center on Silver Springs Boulevard to buy groceries. It wasn't far from where we lived, so she would put Billy in the stroller while Beth toddled at her side. It was also where we bought our groceries.

One time I volunteered to do the grocery shopping for Betty. We had very little money, so I bought some hot dogs and hamburger and other comparatively inexpensive items. When I got in line to check out, a woman was ahead of me in line with all sorts of groceries. I wished I had the money to buy the hams, steaks, and roasts that I saw her unload. Then she pulled out her welfare check and food stamps to pay for the groceries. I couldn't help but get mad.

"Is anyone in your family afflicted?" I asked.

"No, not that it's any of your business," she replied haughtily.

"Well, does anyone work?" I persisted.

"We don't need to work," she informed me. "The government takes care of us."

I'm afraid I wasn't a very good testimony, for I was steamed. "I am afflicted and I have a family. I do work, and you have no right to take my money that I paid in taxes to buy food for your lazy family!"

I was attracting attention by now. The woman couldn't wait to get out of there. The manager walked over to find out what the disturbance was all about. I told him what had happened. He agreed with me, but said there was nothing they could do about it.

When I got home Betty could tell I was upset. "What happened?" she asked.

"Oh, nothing."

"I don't believe that. I can tell you are mad enough to blow a blood vessel." Wives are hard to fool. I told her all about what happened at the grocery store. She wasn't pleased either, but said, "We don't need to worry about it. The Lord gives us what we need." She was right, and I had to ask the Lord's forgiveness for my jealousy and complaining.

We had a lot of good times in our little house. The size of our house didn't keep friends from stopping in to fellowship. Once Rev. and Mrs. Charles Teagle visited, and while my wife was out in the kitchen they asked, "What is your wife's first name?"

"Honey," I told them. I always called her "Honey," or "Mom" because of the children.

"No, that's just what you call her. What is her real name?" For the life of me, I couldn't remember. Here we had been married five years, and I couldn't remember my own wife's name! The Teagles began to laugh. Betty must have overheard, for I could hear her laughing out in the kitchen. I walked back to the kitchen and asked, "Honey, what is your name?"

"William Thomas Maher, my name is Betty!" she exclaimed through her snickers.

We went back into the living room where the Teagles sat. "How long have you two been married?" asked Charles.

"Five years," I said, laughing with them.

"Well, Bill," Charles, said, "allow me to introduce you to your wife of five years. Her name is Betty!"

THE COURAGE AND HOPE HOUR

I continued to minister to the handicapped locally and travel to preach when invited. In 1964 I returned to preach at Bob Jones University. It was my fifth time to speak there. Mr. Jim Ryerson, manager of the university's Christian radio station, put my chapel message on the air during a program called "The Chapel Hour." Many people called in to find out more about this afflicted fellow who preached on the radio. Handicapped people called to see if I had a regular broadcast they could listen to. Mr. Ryerson was amazed at this unusual response. Curious to see what would happen, he broadcast another message I had preached in chapel. This time even more people called. Many asked if I could be on every week, so Mr. Ryerson called me and requested that I go on the air every Sunday morning. I told him I didn't have the money to pay for it, and the handicapped listeners didn't either.

"Well, let's try something," he said. "If you can pay fifteen dollars a month for a weekly fifteen minute broadcast, we'll try to work something out." That was the how "The Courage and Hope Hour" was born on the first Sunday of July 1964.

We trusted the Lord to provide the money for it, and He did. After a couple of years, Mr. Ryerson wrote to tell me that they would continue to broadcast the program each week, but with this difference—I wouldn't have to pay for it anymore. Praise the

Lord! I appreciated the people at the station who were concerned with reaching all people, including the handicapped, for Christ.

GOD SUPPLIES A NEW HOUSE

As the children grew older, Betty and I realized we needed a larger house. I told her we couldn't afford another house, but she said it wouldn't hurt to pray for one. "I would like a new house," she said.

"I'd be happy with just an old one that we could fix up!" I exclaimed.

"I thought you said God can do anything, if it is according to His will," she reminded me. This little wife of mine constantly challenged me to practice what I had been preaching.

"Well, of course He can," I replied, trying sound spiritual. "But he doesn't expect us to ask for foolish things." I knew in my heart I just lacked the faith to pray that way.

"You can pray for an old house if you want, but I am going to pray for a new one," Betty said. "The Lord can give us a new one as well as an old one, and we will be content either way." I had to agree with her wisdom.

We began looking at houses, both old and new. One day Betty said, "You know, we ought to be specific in our prayers. We ought to tell our Father exactly what we want. I am going to pray for three bedrooms, two bathrooms, a living room and dining room, a family room, and, of course, a nice kitchen. And I think I would like old brick on the front. What do you want?"

I never thought about being able to place an order for exactly what I would like, but I said, "I would like a car port, and a large yard would be nice to give us a little more privacy. The two bathrooms would be convenient too." We began to pray with these specific things in mind.

Nothing seemed to be happening in regard to our prayers. I went on the road preaching in the winter of 1964. Then I was home the last two weeks in February. The first day I was back, as had become my custom when I was home, I scanned the newspaper real estate ads. One ad in particular caught my attention. It read: "We trade our new home for your old home." I laughed and told Betty about it. "We ought to call and see what kind of gimmick this is."

"I guess it won't hurt to call," Betty said.

We called and got more information. Although it seemed legitimate, it just seemed too good to be true. We told the salesman about our situation and made an appointment to see him Wednesday morning.

When we walked into the real estate office on Wednesday, the salesman said excitedly, "You are just the kind of people we are looking for. We have a house just for you!" Oh, sure, I thought. "There's only one problem," he continued. "My car is in the shop. If we can use your car, I'll take you to see the house." I agreed, and we drove off. I honestly wasn't expecting much.

As he began directing us to the house, we noticed there were a lot of nice trees in this development. Finally we turned onto N. E. 54th Court. We couldn't believe our eyes! There sat the house that we had prayed for. It was situated on about an acre of ground. It had old brick on the front and a carport. Inside it had everything we wanted except the family room. The men were still working on it. I didn't know what Betty thought, but I was excited.

"Well, preacher, what do you think about this house?" the salesman wanted to know.

"It's everything we prayed for," I replied in awe.

"How about going through with the deal then?" I thought he was going too fast.

"Wait a minute," I objected. "I don't know if we can afford this place. Besides, we want the $3,000 we have invested in our old house on Lynwood Street." I was trying to sound business-like.

"Preacher, we'll give that to you. But what do you think the price of your new house is?" My new house?

"It has to be at least $25,000," I guessed.

"You're way off." He was enjoying this. "Try again."

"I'm sure it can't be less than that," I insisted.

"Okay," he said. "This house is $13,500. We'll take your house and give you the $3,000 for the down payment. Is that all right with you?"

"But you haven't even seen our house." I protested. "And since I am driving, I am going to take you to see it." No one was going to say I hadn't been honest with them.

"Boy, you sure are hard to please," the salesman chuckled.

As we drove in the driveway at Lynwood Street, Betty and I were both praying for the Lord's will to be done. "This house has a new roof," I told the salesman, "but everything else in the house has problems," and I began to enumerate them.

"I appreciate your honesty," he said, "but we still want to make the deal with you." We drove back to the real estate office. I still couldn't believe it.

"Hold it," I said. "What does the owner of the business think about this deal?"

"Will you be home tonight?" the salesman asked. "I'll give you a call and tell you what my boss says. That should put your mind at ease."

"Fine, but please call before 6 p.m. I'm preaching at prayer meeting at Central Baptist Church."

Later Betty got supper ready and fed the children, but she and I were too excited to eat. I had never received a phone call as important as the one we were expecting. Finally at 5:45 p.m. the phone rang. It was the real estate salesman.

"Preacher, can you be here tomorrow morning by nine? We'd like to sign the papers. The boss says everything is okay!"

"We'll be there!" I said while I silently praised the Lord. "Thank you very much for calling." I hung up the phone and gave Betty a bear hug. She was laughing, but with tears running down her cheeks. I guess I was too. Beth and Billy saw our tears and both started to cry, thinking something was wrong. "No, no, there's nothing wrong," Betty told them. "We're just happy that we are going to get a new house," and she began to tell them about it.

I have no idea what I said at prayer meeting that night, except I know that I told them how God had given us a new house, and that we would be moving in the very near future.

The next morning we arrived at the real estate office with

the deed to our property ready to sign for the new home. The salesman was waiting for us. He made us comfortable and then went to see his boss. "Boy, they are taking a long time with the paperwork," I remarked to Betty.

"Just be patient, Bill," Betty said. "It cannot be done in a few seconds." But I could tell she was as nervous as I was.

Finally the salesman came out. "We had to work out a couple of problems and talk to the people at the bank that holds the mortgage on your old property, but everything turned out fine," he said. "Now we can start signing all the necessary papers."

We sat down and starting filling out the paperwork. "Preacher, when are you going to be back on the road preaching?" the salesman asked.

"I have to get back on the road next week," I replied.

"How would you like to get your family into your new house before you leave? We have taken the workers off all the other houses to work on yours."

"That would be wonderful! I really appreciate this." I also thought it was wonderful when he said "your house."

We went back to our old house feeling kind of sad, but not too sad to want to stay! Billy Cordrey gave me permission to use his truck to move our belongings to our new house. I had the electricity turned on and the gas tank filled at the new house. Now I had to get the telephone hooked up. I went down to the phone company and talked to one of the women who worked there.

"Mr. Maher, I'm afraid you cannot have telephone service until the development is complete," she curtly informed me.

"That cannot be!" I protested. "I will be going on the road, and I can't leave my wife behind with two small children and no telephone."

The young woman wouldn't budge. She had no sympathy. She acted like she owned the company. By this time I was steamed at her inflexibility. I knew the department manager from church, so I walked over to his office and told him about my problem and what the young woman had told me. He got really angry at this young woman. He marched to her desk and spoke to her. I couldn't hear what was said, but I saw the young woman's face turn red. The manager came back and told me I would have telephone service by the end of the week.

As I left I stopped by the woman's desk and said, "You should never talk to the Maher like you did today." She apologized profusely, saying she didn't know I was the mayor! I walked out chuckling.

The very next day my back went out. I knew I couldn't do the heavy moving work. *Lord,* I complained, *don't you know I have to move? Why did this have to happen now?*

I went over to the Cordreys and told them I wouldn't be using their truck, for I would have to make other arrangements. Betty Cordrey recommended that I talk with a Christian mover whom she knew. I went to see him at his office right away.

"Brother Maher!" he exclaimed when he saw me, as though we were old friends.

"Do you know me?" I asked.

"Yes. I heard you preach at our church. You did a good job. What can we do for you?" I told him about my situation and inquired about how much it would cost for him to move us.

"Brother Maher, I'll give you the use of the moving van if you will pay the workers. It will cost you forty-five dollars."

"That's wonderful!" I replied. "But I need to move this coming Saturday."

"That's no problem," he said. "The men will be there."

I went home and told Betty and the children that we would be in our new house by Saturday night. We were all very excited. When we went to bed Friday night, no one could sleep.

The men arrived on Saturday morning and swarmed through our house, packing and loading our belongings. In no time at all it was taken to our new house. Soon everything was unloaded and in place. *If I was doing this, it would have taken all day,* I thought. *Thank you, Lord, for the bad back. You always know what's best.* That night we were in the new house praising the Lord for His goodness and provision for us.

I left the next morning. While I was on the road, Betty would write in her letters that we had this feature or that item in the house. Of course, I didn't know, for I was there only one night. She said there was still a paper hanger working at the house, and she thought he was the slowest worker she had ever seen.

Before I returned home I had time to think about what happened. I began to wonder how we had ever gotten a loan on the house. We never visited a bank or had a credit check.

After I got home I went to see the real estate salesman to find out how this had happened. He was glad to see me, but wondered if anything was wrong.

"No," I told him. "I have just been wondering how we got the loan for our house."

"I think it is time you met the man who arranged everything for you," he said. "He heard you give your testimony and wanted to do something special for you and your family. He was born in Japan, where his parents were missionaries." That day the man introduced me to Mr. Don Phaff. I sincerely thanked Mr. Phaff, but he gave God the glory for allowing him to help us. That was the only time I ever met him.

BETTY LEARNS TO DRIVE

There was a problem at our new location that we hadn't foreseen. Betty didn't drive. At our old house she had been able to walk to the grocery store, but now she was dependent on others to take her where she needed to go. Betty decided it was time she learned to drive. Since I had taught others, I thought it shouldn't be hard to teach my wife. Was I ever wrong!

I had heard the old joke that if you want a divorce, attempt to teach your wife how to drive. But I didn't believe it was true. My wife was a very sweet girl, and I was a very patient man. We started out fine, but then she would not do what I told her to do. She would just tell me not to howl at her. "I'm not howling!" I would howl, "I'm trying to tell you what to do, but you won't pay attention!" Somehow our marriage survived until she got the permit that allowed her to drive if another licensed driver was with her.

When I had a preaching engagement in Pensacola, I took

the bus so she could have the car. When I came home Betty met me at the bus station. No one was with her. I was very surprised. "What are you doing driving here with just the children? Don't you remember that you can't drive without a licensed driver with you?" No reply, just a smile.

I put my luggage in the trunk, and she got in on the driver's side. "Hold it," I demanded. "I am going to drive."

"You are with me, so I can drive," she reminded me.

"Oh. That's right. You go ahead and I can see how you are doing with your driving," said the pompous instructor. I was still trying to figure out why she drove by herself to the bus station. It wasn't like her to disobey the law.

After we got home and I unpacked, I sat in the reclining chair in the living room and again asked Betty why she drove alone to the bus station. She never said anything. She just smiled. I hate it when she does that. She put a small card under my nose and kept on smirking. It was her driver's license!

"How and when did you get this?"

"When you were gone I got Frankie Green to take me over to the driver testing place. I took the test and passed," she said proudly.

"Great!" I responded, thankful that I wouldn't have to "howl" through any more driving lessons.

"It was a good thing you knew the fellow who gave the driving test," she said.

"Who do you mean?" I wondered.

"Well, when the fellow saw my name he asked if my husband was the preacher who stopped at the 76 service station on Silver Springs Boulevard. I said 'yes.' He said he knew you from when he used to work there before getting this job. Anyway, it was a good thing. He noticed I couldn't parallel park very well, and he had me return on Saturday to try it over. Only this time, he wasn't going to be out there watching me. I passed."

From that time on Betty became the one who ran all of the errands to the post office and other places. She took care of the paper work, sent out receipts, and mailed my prayer letters. She became a tremendous help, allowing me to do so much more than I would have been able to do otherwise. I couldn't do without her, and I thank the Lord for sending me such a great helper in the Lord's work. To me she is the epitome of the virtuous woman described in Proverbs 31.

Water Under the Bridge

Over time our support level increased, and God often worked in strange ways to cause churches to support us. Once I was asked to come to the Bill Rice Ranch to speak for a week to the deaf. The main speaker was Rev. Bob Keyes from Texas. He heard me speak in the morning service, and afterward we talked for a little while. The next day he told me he had to return home right away because of the death of one of his church members. "Tell me everything about yourself and your ministry in ten minutes," he said, and I did.

A month after I returned home, a check for twenty-five dollars arrived from Galilean Baptist Church in Dallas, Texas. Betty called it to my attention and asked if I knew why it came. She knew I had never been to Texas. I told her I didn't know why it came, I was just thankful it did. I forgot about it until another check arrived the next month. Now I had to solve the mystery. I wrote to the church and learned that the pastor was Rev. Bob Keyes.

The checks kept coming every month. After about three years I decided I had better visit the church, and maybe some other churches there would have me. My dear wife said that maybe I should stay away, for they may stop supporting us if they ever heard me preach.

I asked Rev. Keyes for directions to the church once I reached Dallas. He wrote, "When you cross a bridge with a river under it, you'll take your next left."

After driving two days in my Nash Rambler, I reached Dallas. I crossed several bridges, but none had a river under it. I turned around and crossed these bridges several times, looking in vain for a river. I thought I was lost. Then things got worse. A policeman pulled me over. I thought I was going to get a ticket, although I didn't know what I might have done wrong.

"Are you all right?" the policeman asked. "I've watched you drive over this bridge time and again."

"I'm fine, Officer," I replied. "I'm trying to find the bridge with the river under it." I showed him the letter with the directions. He looked at it and burst out laughing.

"I'm sorry the state of Texas isn't cooperating this time of year. It hasn't rained in a while, so the river has dried up. That's why there's no water under the bridge." He and I had a good laugh. Then he led me off to the church.

When I got to church, I told Pastor Keyes that the next time I came to Dallas, please be sure to have some water under the bridge! Pastor Keyes treated me like royalty and made me feel like I was his favorite missionary. He arranged for me to preach at several other churches in the area, such as Lavon Drive Baptist Church in Garland, where Dr. Gary Coleman is pastor, and Mineral Heights Baptist Church in Greenville, Texas, where Brother Jack Power was the pastor. I appreciated the confidence Pastor Keyes had in me, and over the years we have often laughed about the need to have water under the bridge when I come to Dallas.

10

THE JOYS OF FATHERHOOD

As the kids were growing up, I would often take one or both of them with me to various meetings. If I had meetings in Ohio, I would take them to my sister's house to visit their Aunt Lenore and Uncle Bill while I preached in area churches. Otherwise, they accompanied me around the state of Florida, where most of my meetings were. Once I took Billy to Jacksonville when I preached there. We stayed in a motel, and I took Billy to see various attractions. When we came home, he teased his sister about all the places he had been and she hadn't. We tried to make him stop, but that was like trying to keep the sun from rising every morning. I decided to take Beth with me the next time I went out so she could say she had seen some things too.

Over the Labor Day weekend I had a Sunday night service, and I decided that would be a good time to take Beth along. Betty and I wanted to surprise her. We packed everything in the trunk on Saturday night before we were to leave. We came right home after Sunday school. Betty said to Beth, "Will you go with Daddy to get me something for my headache? He will need your help picking out the right medicine." Beth was eager to help and I'm sure she wondered why we didn't ask her to change from her Sunday best dress to everyday clothes, but she didn't question anything. After we went to the drug store, I mentioned that we should go by the post office and check our mail while we were out. She was willing to help, but I could see she was puzzled. We never checked our mail on Sunday. As we drove away from the post office, we were close to the main highway and I told her the car needed gas.

She looked at me, excitement and comprehension in her eyes. "Daddy, are we going to go to Jacksonville like Billy did?" she asked.

"Yes, honey," I answered.

"But Daddy, we need our clothes!"

"Honey," I replied, "we put everything we need in the trunk last night so we could surprise you."

"Then I will take Mother's place," she proudly proclaimed. She moved over next to me on the seat and took my hand, like her mother did. Such moments in a father's life pass all too quickly.

We got to the motel and rested, then went on to the church where I preached. The next day I took Beth to places where Billy had never been so she would have some experiences to tell him about. We visited Marineland, and various places in St. Augustine. About six p.m. I noticed that Beth had grown quiet.

"What the matter, honey? Are you all right?"

"Yes, Daddy. I'm just real tired."

"You're not homesick, are you?" I was sure she was.

"Oh, yes, Daddy. I miss Mother and even Billy. Can we go home now?" she pleaded.

I laughed and assured her we would head home.

"I'm going to get in back now," she said.

I knew she wanted to take a nap, so before she fell asleep I asked, "Are you going to tease Billy about where you have been?"

"I sure am, and it's going to be fun."

And tease Billy she did. He didn't like this at all, but Betty and I did not stop Beth until we were sure Billy would not tease his sister again.

FRIENDS IN THE MINISTRY

I made many long friendships with pastors during my ministry. One of my good friends was Rev. Charles Teagles, pastor of Crusade Baptist Church in Ohio. I was having meetings with him one time when he took me downtown to a store in Akron. As we were leaving, we met a pastor, whom Rev. Teagles introduced to me as Rev. Dean Henry, pastor of Brown Street Baptist Church there in Akron.

"I'm mad at you!" said Rev. Henry. I sure was surprised, for we had only been introduced.

"Why is that?" I asked him.

"I am angry because you have never been to my church!" he said loudly.

Two can play this game, I thought. "I have a good reason for not preaching at your church," I said, raising my voice.

He bristled. "Why?"

"You have never invited me," I said softly, and smiled at him.

A grin spread across his face. "You're right," he admitted. He reached into his pocket and pulled out a date book to see when I could be with him. "Our missions conference will be in April of next year. Can you be with us then?" he asked.

"I think so." I pulled out my calendar and checked to make sure I could, then everything was settled.

The following April I stayed at the Henrys' home when I was there for the conference. We got to be great friends, but when I left, I didn't expect him to have me again soon.

A year later I was preaching at a four-day Bible conference for Rev. Lanny Akers in Cleveland, Ohio. On Wednesday of that week, Rev. Henry called to see if I would be available on the coming Friday, Saturday, and Sunday. I told him I had Friday and Saturday nights off, but on Sunday I started a week of revival meetings not far from his church.

"I'll come and pick you up on Friday afternoon," he said, as if everything was settled.

"Wait a minute. Why are you coming for me, and where are you taking me?" I asked.

"Oh, I forgot to mention that one of our missionary guests cannot be with us, so I called your wife to find out where you were so I could have you come in his place. So I'll see you on Friday."

"Hold it! I'm having meetings at another church starting on Sunday morning," I reminded him.

"That will work out fine," he assured me. "I'll give you some time Friday and Saturday night to speak, and again in the adult Sunday school class. Then I will run you over to the other church in time for you to preach. See you on Friday," he said, and hung up before I could say "yes" or "no" or raise any more objections.

Everything worked out, and after I spoke to the Sunday school class he took me over to the other church. On the way I told him a deacon had let me know when their missions conference was scheduled the next year, so he wouldn't have to bother calling me. I would just show up at his church at the right time.

The next year I drove up to his church when the missions conference was scheduled to start. I walked in the first service and said to Rev. Henry, "Here I am. Where am I staying?"

The startled expression on Rev. Henry's face was priceless. "What are you doing here?" a deacon demanded.

"Never mind," Rev. Henry said to him. "He said he would show up this year, but I didn't think he would have the nerve to do it." He began to chuckle. "Now I guess I'll have to put up with him."

We had a great time that year. I kept being with them annually until Rev. Henry told me he didn't want me at the missions conference any more. Instead, he decided I should start having revival meetings for him in the fall! I continued to do this until Rev. Henry retired after forty years as the pastor of Brown Street Baptist Church. I miss the fun we had serving the Lord together.

CHAPLAIN MAHER

A few days after I returned home I received a phone call from Chief Kenneth Alvarez of the Ocala police department asking me to come in. He mentioned he had something important to talk over with me. I was very puzzled over what this could be about. I had never been to the police station before. Could I have done something wrong?

At the appointed day I arrived at Chief Alvarez's office. He gave me a warm welcome, for which I was relieved.

"Would you like a cup of coffee?" he asked.

"Uh, no thank you." It was rare for me to turn down a cup of coffee, but I wasn't going to relax until I knew what he wanted. We sat down, and he started in.

"Brother Maher, I'll come right to the point. I'd like to know something. When you preachers come down here to preach to the prisoners, why doesn't anyone talk to the officers? Do they have to steal, kill, or rape before they can get saved? Now I'm not criticizing you personally, but people like you come into the jail all the time and never talk to my employees."

I didn't know what to say. "To tell you the truth," I replied, "I never thought about it before. What would you like for me to do about this?"

"I want you to ride with my boys and tell them about getting saved," he replied.

He doesn't realize what he's asking, I thought. He has got to know I don't do this kind of thing. I am afflicted and am not physically able to do this. He must have read my mind.

"I know what you're thinking. You're saying to yourself that you are not able to do this because you are handicapped. But I heard your testimony when you spoke at the Christian businessmen's luncheon, and I said to myself, 'This is the fellow I need.' You see, some of my people have handicapped children.

"We have a police chaplain," he went on, "but he never shows up. I want you to minister to my people. Will you do it?"

I gulped. "It seems like a wonderful opportunity. I would like to try it. When would you want me to start?"

"Right now! I'll call Lt. Parker and have him take you for a ride around town to introduce you to the men. And every Friday you are home, I'd like for you to ride that night with one of the men."

I gulped again. "I'd better call my wife so she won't worry about me. She was curious about why you called me down here." I made the call, and Betty couldn't believe this tremendous opportunity the Lord had given me.

I went for a ride with Lt. Parker and met some of the men. They were very suspicious of me. I couldn't blame them. Friday night came, and I knew I would face a test. I was paired with a mean sergeant from Asheville, North Carolina. When we got in the car, he said, "Don't try to talk religion with me, preacher."

We drove in silence for a while. Then something happened that made him curse and swear. I began talking to him about the Lord. "Didn't I tell you I don't want to hear about your religion?" he reminded me.

"Yes, you did tell me," I replied. "But if you are going to curse, I'm going to preach." That's the way it went for the next several hours-he would curse, and I would preach. Finally, about 1 a.m., I noticed he had become silent. I glanced over at him and was surprised to see tears rolling down his cheeks. We were stopped at a traffic light when I asked him, "Don't you think it's time you got saved?"

"Yes, but I can't go to church at this time of the morning."

"You don't need to go to church to be saved," I told him. "You can accept Christ right here under this traffic light."

The next thing I knew his head was bowed and his lips were moving. Then he looked up and shouted, "I did it!" He roared away from the intersection with a big smile on his face.

"What did you do?" I inquired.

"I did what you said. I let Jesus Christ into my heart back there at the traffic light like you said I could. I can't wait to tell my wife!" he exclaimed.

I heard no more cursing that night.

When we returned to the squad room, the rest of the men were eager to hear how the mean sergeant handled the preacher. "Hey, what happened? Did you tell him off?" a man asked.

The mean sergeant glared at the group of men and said, "If one of you fellows makes fun of him or doesn't listen to him, you are going to have trouble with me!"

"What in the world has gotten into you?" one man asked.

"You know that light at Silver Springs Boulevard and Magnolia? Well, I got saved there tonight."

"Aw, come on, Sarge, you've got to be kidding," said one man.

"No, I'm not. Rev. Maher is just who we need to help us. I'm all for him, and I'm going to thank the chief for getting him." I knew I was in. The following week the chief called me into his office and expressed his gratitude for what the Lord did. He soon presented me with a police chaplain badge.

After I had been riding with the police for a while, one day I went to get a haircut. I was sitting in the barber chair when Sheriff Willis walked by and spotted me through the window. In he came.

"Rev. Maher, why are you riding with the city police and not with my deputies?" he asked.

"Have you ever asked me to?"

"Uh, no." Then he said to the barber, "How long will it be before you're finished cutting Rev. Maher's hair?"

"Just a few minutes. Why?"

"Because I want him to come over to our department and get

acquainted with our boys," said Sheriff Willis.

After my haircut I went over to the sheriff's department. The door to Sheriff Willis's office was open. He saw me and motioned for me to come in.

"Well, Rev. Maher, I hear you're riding with the city police on Friday nights. The chief over there likes what you do for the men. I'd like for you to ride with my boys on Saturday nights when you are in town. Can you do that?"

"Yes sir," I replied. "I'd like that very much."

Now I was really getting into police work! Friday nights I rode with the city policemen, and Saturday nights I rode with the sheriff's deputies. It was a time of learning about the sin in which other people lived. It was also a time of learning about the law enforcement officers too. I began to understand how they could at times be so cold and cynical. The officers often saw the hypocrisy of professing Christians, and some of them would try to use that against me. I tried to defend these Christians until I learned that what the officers said was often true. It angered me that these Christians had such poor testimonies that they hindered or prevented lost men from coming to Christ.

For example, I accompanied an officer to a bar where two women were about to fight with knives. After we were inside, I recognized a deacon from a nearby church. We separated the two women and put them in the back seat of the squad car. "Just a minute," I told the officer. "I want to talk to a fellow I saw in there. Then I went back inside. I approached the table where the man sat holding a paper in front of his face. I knocked the paper out of his hand and demanded, "What are you doing in here?" There were empty beer bottles on the table.

"Just resting," he said sheepishly.

I was angry. "I'll bet your wife doesn't know you're here, and I know the church doesn't know it."

He got defensive and tried to justify what he was doing. Finally he asked, "What do you expect me to do?"

"Resign as a deacon and confess your sins to God. You need to start being a good husband to your wife and a good father to your children." I turned and walked out.

The officer had followed me and watched across the room. "Well, preacher, you just saw what we see all the time. People talk about their religion but they sure don't live it."

I couldn't argue with him, and I had a lot to overcome in witnessing to him after that.

When Don Moreland became the new sheriff, I continued riding with the deputies throughout the twenty years he served in that office. I enjoyed getting to know the men and learning things about the people in our community and their needs.

A few years later the city councilmen decided to build a new police department building, and likewise the county commissioners voted to build a new sheriff's department. In both instances additional personnel were needed. I challenged Chief Alvarez and Sheriff Moreland to consider hiring the handicapped for certain jobs.

"We can't," they said. "We need able-bodied people."

"To answer the phone?" I objected. "Handicapped people have a brain. How able-bodied do you have to be to answer the phone? Just give them a try. You'll be surprised at what the handicapped can do."

Chief Alvarez decided to take a chance. He hired Jim Polk to handle the radio department. Jim did so well that he soon became the chief's assistant. Chief Alvarez then hired other handicapped people who also performed well, and one even started handling the department's finances. The city and county paid for some to go to college, and one was even sent to the F.B.I. for further training. Remembering all the prejudice I had encountered over the years, I was grateful to our local law enforcement agencies for hiring the afflicted.

Hidden Treasure

One day in 1981 a letter from Greenville, South Carolina, appeared in my post office box. It was from Rev. John Vaughn, pastor of Faith Baptist Church. Rev. Vaughn's letter mentioned that he had heard about me from a friend of his while attending Bob Jones University. He asked me if I could come to the church for a week-end meeting, which included preaching five times on Sunday. Five times on Sunday? What kind of a church was this that had five services on Sunday? He also mentioned that he had a handicapped daughter, but he didn't mention specifically what her handicap was.

I sent a letter back to him telling him I could come and that I looked forward to being with him and his people. I gave him my expected time of arrival at the Greenville airport, but I realized that he had no idea how to recognize me, nor I him.

When I arrived at the Greenville airport, a very tired-looking young man approached me. "Are you Rev. William Maher?" he asked.

I assured him I was the man he was looking for, and we picked up my luggage and loaded it in the car. On the way to his house, Rev. Vaughn asked me if I had heard about the fire at his house in 1978. I hadn't, so he began to tell me the story about how Brenda, his wife, had rescued his two-year-old daughter Becky from the fire. Both were severely burned and were still undergoing medical treatment. I admit that when I heard the story, I wasn't looking forward to meeting Brenda and Becky.

When we arrived, Brenda came out of the house to meet me. I noticed that her face, hands, and feet were badly scarred, but there was a big smile on her face. I was afraid to shake her hand too hard for fear of hurting her. Brenda was looking me over to see if I was all right to meet her children, especially Becky. We went inside. I must have passed inspection, for they brought Becky out and placed her on my lap. There was an immediate rapport between me and this little burn-scarred girl.

After preaching on Friday and Saturday, I was getting ready to preach five times on Sunday, twice in the morning and three times in the evening. The reason was that the church had grown from 40 people to about 1000 in the same little building.

"By the way, Brother Maher, you can preach one message at the two morning services, and the same message three times in the evening," Rev. Vaughn told me.

"Now you tell me," I said. "You could tape my message in the first service in the morning and evening, and I can go back to my room and rest."

After supper on Saturday, Rev. Vaughn told me he was concerned that Becky was old enough to go to school, but he didn't know if she could go to a regular school.

"No!" I told him emphatically. "Remember, she is already suffering physically, and if she goes to a regular school the other children will make fun of her and she will suffer emotionally too. I know; I went through that and would not wish anyone else to have to endure that kind of cruelty."

"Then what are we supposed to do? There's nothing wrong with Becky's mind. She has to go to some kind of school. Brenda isn't able to school her. Do you have any ideas?"

"Sure," I replied. "The idea already came to me and I have been praying about the right time to tell you. You should start a school for the handicapped, and I will help you."

"What? I can't do that!" he objected. "I don't know anything about starting a school. Pastoring the church takes all of my time anyway."

I smiled at him and asked, "Do you have a better idea? If so, I'd like to hear it. But I think the Lord put us together to get this school started."

"No way!" he exclaimed. "I just can't do it. There must be another way."

"Well, I'm going to bed. I have a long day tomorrow. I have the peace of the Lord that this is what you must do, so I am going to rest in the Lord while He works on you. Before I leave, let me know what you decide to do. Good night."

Sunday was indeed a long day. We didn't have time to talk more about the special education school. Finally the fifth service was over. I was really tired. Now I understood why Rev. Vaughn looked so tired. I was glad my plane wasn't leaving until later in the day on Monday so I could rest. We sat down to a meal that evening, and afterward I asked Rev. Vaughn, "Have you thought any more about starting that school?"

Brenda looked at him but said nothing. I knew she was praying too. Rev. Vaughn looked serious but gave me no reply.

After breakfast on Monday morning, I made another appeal. "One more time, what will you do about the school for Becky and children like her? I want to know if I will be helping or praying."

"Brother Bill, I haven't slept since we talked about it Saturday night. You knew I wouldn't, didn't you?"

"Yep," I replied. "I asked the Lord not to let you rest until you came to a decision."

"Why me?" he groaned.

"Why not you?"

"Do you promise to help me?" he implored.

"I said I would."

"Then when can we get started?"

"I will be back in time to get started by this fall, even if Becky is the only student," I assured him. Rev. Vaughn did most of the work while I provided mostly encouragement. I soon became "Dad" to Rev. Vaughn and "Uncle Bill" to the Vaughn children. The result of our labors was Hidden Treasure Christian School for the mentally and physically handicapped. The school's name comes from II Corinthians 4:7. Becky was one of the two students that fall.

Today Hidden Treasure Christian School has more than sixty students, with a waiting list. Students learn not to be bitter about having a handicap, but rather to realized that they have everything they need to do God's will for their life. The school operates in the small, old Faith Baptist Church buildings where I first preached five times in one day. The school could help many more students except for the limitations of its facilities. Therefore Hidden Treasure is raising funds to build a new school on property provided by Faith Baptist Church that will enable it to help more than 100 handicapped children. I have served on the board of the school since it was founded. And best of all, Becky has graduated and is now attending a Christian college, thanks to the education she received at Hidden Treasure.

A MISSION TRIP TO THE CARIBBEAN

My first trip to a foreign mission field took place in 1971. I never dreamed that such an opportunity would arise for a fellow like me. I was in a missions conference at a Baptist church in Norfolk, Virginia. One of the missionaries was Brother Freeman Goodge, who labored in the Virgin Islands. When he learned that I had never been to that area, he asked me accompany him when he returned to the field.

We planned to meet at the Miami airport to fly to Puerto Rico and then on to St. Thomas. We would spend the night there, then continue on to St. Martin and on to the small island where he lived. "Don't wear anything fancy," Freeman instructed me. "Just bring five or six changes. We have a washing machine in case your clothing gets dusty. We don't wear suits in the islands." I liked that.

I returned home and told my family about the unexpected opportunity the Lord had given me. They were excited for me and helped me pack. I was going to the Virgin Islands for a month! I had never done anything like this before.

I flew from Ocala to Miami. This was a big airport, and I was concerned about finding my way around. As I tried to figure out which way to go to get to the right airline to find Brother Goodge, I wondered if he had left without me. After wandering all over the airport, I finally heard someone yell, "Over here!" It was Brother Goodge. We boarded the plane, and I still couldn't believe that I had the privilege to visit, and especially to preach in, a foreign country.

We reached Puerto Rico, and then boarded another plane for the short hop to St. Thomas. "I might as well warn you," Brother Goodge said. "This plane will appear to land in the sea. The runway at St. Thomas extends out into the Caribbean, and it seems like you are landing in the water. At the other end of the runway is a mountain, so the runway had to be extended into the water to be long enough. And another thing: you will see smoke coming out from under the plane when we land, but don't worry about that. It's just the brakes."

I figured Brother Goodge was teasing me, but sure enough, the plane appeared to land out in the middle of the Caribbean Sea! Smoke poured from beneath the plane as the pilot braked hard. I was holding on to my seat for dear life! After the plane stopped and made a sharp turn, I saw the mountain at the end of the runway. I was glad I wouldn't have to land there often.

We spent the night there with a missionary and his family before heading for St. Martin and the small island of Anguilla. We made plans for meetings each night, then decided to get a good night's sleep. Sleep? I was too excited to sleep. I still couldn't believe I was to hold revival meetings on a foreign mission field. A cool wind was blowing in from the sea, and before I knew it morning had arrived and it was time to get up.

After breakfast, we went to visit people around the island to invite them to our special meetings. We met several handicapped people on the island, and invited them as well. At night we could hear the drums of the demon worshipers, but I still preached every night for two weeks with good results.

The missionaries decided that I should be used on other islands too. We headed back to St. Thomas. This time when we landed and headed right for that mountain at the end of the runway, I closed my eyes! The people on the island treated me like royalty. Meetings were planned for my remaining two weeks in the islands. I even preached at the Bible institute on the island, where I was greatly blessed by these people who loved the Lord and were preparing to serve Him wherever He wanted them. It was a great privilege, and truly my joy was unspeakable.

Before returning home, I stopped in Puerto Rico for a couple of days of meetings. Soon my time had come to an end, and I was eager to get home and report on all the Lord had done. It was still unbelievable that someone afflicted such as me could go on a trip like this. I was thankful that the Lord did not recognize any limitations for the afflicted.

I Go to Brazil

Once when I was at a missions conference, one of the missionaries, Bill Phillips, asked me to come to São Paulo, Brazil, where he was going. He wanted me to come after he had been to language school to learn Portuguese. I didn't know what to say. I thought that maybe he was inviting me just to be kind. I told the Lord that if someone else would ask me to go, I would take it as a sign from Him that I should do it.

A while after this I was in one of the conferences at Brown Street Baptist Church. Albert and Doris Johnson, missionaries in Fortaleza, Brazil, asked me to come down to be with them. The Lord was saying to me, *All right, I've given you another invitation. Are you going to obey?*

Yes, sir. Now I knew I was going to go to Brazil, and my heart was flooded with joy. I told everyone I met, "Hey, have you heard the good news? I'm going to Brazil. The missionaries have asked me to come and preach for them, and they want me to help them reach the afflicted for Christ. I need help to get there. Will you help me?" I sent letters to everyone I knew seeking help to pay the expenses.

Finally the money was raised. I had my passport in hand. I had all the necessary immunization shots. The local travel agency made arrangements for me to fly from Ocala to Miami and on to São Paulo. After two weeks in São Paulo, I would fly to Fortaleza, in the northern part of Brazil. I was very excited to leave.

At last I left on my all-night flight. The devil began to work on me. All sorts of doubts began to enter my mind. What if this Catholic country would not let a Baptist preacher in? I had to trust in the Lord and see what would happen.

One thing the missionaries had said to me was that I had to be initiated into Brazil by drinking some Brazilian coffee. So what, I thought. I have been drinking coffee for years. At about midnight, the flight attendant asked me if I wanted *café*. *Of course he means coffee,* I said to myself. *I'll go ahead and drink some now, and when I arrive in Sao Paulo I can tell the missionaries that I already had some of their Brazilian coffee.* "Yes," I told the attendant.

"Would you like the small cup or the large one, sir?" he asked.

I was a coffee drinker, so I said, "I'll take the big one." Several Brazilians on board had turned to see who was ordering a large cup of their coffee.

"Would you like cream and sugar?" the attendant said with a smile as he poured my steaming cup.

"No, I drink it black." Several other Brazilians now turned to see who was talking.

The flight attendant offered *café* to the Brazilian man across the aisle. He took a small cup and put lots of milk and sugar in it. *Uh-oh. I'm in trouble!*

By this time it seemed like everyone on the plane was watching me. I took a drink. Strong is not the word for this stuff. I don't think

Superman could drink Brazilian coffee black, but Bill Maher was doing it. I didn't want to embarrass myself in front of all those people, so I drank it all. Soon everyone tired of watching me and fell asleep. But not me! I felt like I was vibrating! If I closed my eyes they popped open again.

Finally the sun rose after my sleepless night. We had breakfast, and this time I asked for American coffee. We landed at the Sao Paulo airport, which was not far from where Bill Phillips and his family lived. I walked off the plane and began to follow the other passengers. Two Catholic priests were walking in front of me. *The Brazilians will let them in and tell me to go home,* I thought.

A young lady working with the check-in was coming down the line of new arrivals I was standing in, asking where they came from. She talked to the priests, and then spoke to me in Portuguese. I shook my head.

"I'm an American. Can you speak English?" I asked her. She turned and called another lady who spoke English. She asked to see my passport, and asked what I did for a living. *Now I'm in trouble,* I thought.

"I'm a preacher," I said.

"What kind?" she inquired.

"Baptist."

With a smile the lady took my hand and said, "Come with me, please." She took me to the man stamping the passports and said something in Portuguese. He stamped my passport and handed it back to me. "Welcome to our country," she said pleasantly. She showed me where to go to collect my luggage. When I picked up my luggage the man at the counter looked at my passport and waved me on with a smile. That was all there was to it. I was thrilled to get through without any problems. Praise the Lord!

Bill Phillips was waiting for me when I exited the terminal. He wanted to treat me to a cold drink, and while we drank our Coca-Colas, he noticed my patriotic eyes-red, white, and blue!

"You drank some *café,* didn't you?"

"Yes," I replied, "and when will I ever get to sleep again?"

"When did you drink it?"

"About midnight, as I recall."

"Hmm. I doubt you'll be able to sleep before three o'clock this afternoon," he informed me. It was 9:30 a.m. then. "At least you have your initiation over with," Bill teased.

We went to his house where I got reacquainted with his wife and two sons. My bedroom was upstairs right across from the bathroom. *Great!* I thought. I decided to get a shower. I got in and turned on the water. It was cold so I turned on the other knob. After running a while, the water was still cold. I heard Bill call out from the hallway, "I forgot to tell you, Bill. There's no hot water. Both knobs are cold."

"No kidding," I called out. I learned to take a cold shower in less than a minute!

I went back downstairs. Although the house was beautiful, Bill informed me that very few homes had hot water. They would soon get it, but not before I left, of course.

"Do you sleep with your mouth open?" Bill asked me.

"I don't know. I never stayed awake to find out. Why do you ask?"

"Every home down here has cockroaches. They come out at night, so I suggest you sleep with your mouth closed or we won't have to feed you breakfast in the morning." I hoped he was teasing me and exaggerating, but I had thought the same thing about Brazilian coffee.

About three p.m. I finally started to feel sleepy. I slept for three hours, and I was so exhausted I had no idea if I slept with my mouth open or not.

Some of the other missionaries came over to be with us for supper. I met the Joneses, the Frays, the Santos family, and others. We spent some time planning what I was to do. We had a good time of fellowship together. At ten p.m. I was ready for bed. Someone reminded me to keep my mouth shut because of the cockroaches. I really didn't believe them.

About four a.m. I awoke. I grabbed my flashlight to see for myself if there were really cockroaches. I clicked it on, and cockroaches scurried everywhere, even on my bed! Some of them were half as big as my hand! You can be sure I slept with my mouth closed the whole time I was in Brazil.

The next day I got to work. Brother Marvin Fray arranged for me to preach in the special hospital for the afflicted. It was run by the Roman Catholic church, but they allowed the Protestants to have services. We took advantage of the opportunity, and as a result some of the handicapped were saved. As I was walking around talking to some of these people individually through an interpreter, one of the nuns beckoned to me from a corner of the room. I found that the nuns could speak and understand English very well.

"Can I do what they are doing?" she asked.

"What do you think they are doing?" I wanted to know if she understood what I had been preaching.

"They are asking Jesus Christ to come into their hearts and save them. I want to do that too."

I assured her she could. She bowed her head without crossing herself and asked Christ Jesus to save her. She wiped a tear from the corner of her eye, and smiled a big smile. "Thank you," she said, and walked away.

I continued talking with afflicted individuals, and yet another nun appeared and motioned for me to follow her. We stopped around the corner. "Look," she started in, "I know I am a Catholic nun, but I would gladly become afflicted if I could be saved like those handicapped people did."

"But without Christ, you are afflicted."

"You are right. I go through all of this ritual but I have no peace. Can I be saved right here, right now?"

"Yes," I assured her. "Simply confess that you are a sinner, and ask Jesus Christ to come into your heart and save you."

She bowed her head and prayed, "A sinner I am, and I know I have a need to be saved. I accept Jesus Christ as my Savior."

I had no doubts of the two nuns' sincerity, for they showed up at my meetings later in the week. They said publicly that they wanted to be identified with the "born again" people.

Besides preaching at the hospitals and churches, I was the main speaker at a retreat for the pastors and missionaries and their families. Bill Phillips took me to the campground. I was expecting a primitive camp and living conditions, but to my surprise they had beautiful buildings—cabins, a chapel and dining hall, and a house where the camp director, Rev. Shoaf and his wife lived. I would be staying at their house, and when Bill dropped me off he told me he was jealous, for the Shoafs' house had hot water. I became excited about the prospect of taking hot showers.

The Shoafs' job was to keep everything operating smoothly. I noticed Mrs. Shoaf acted a little flustered. She was very kind and helpful, but I knew something just wasn't quite right. Finally I asked her if there was something I could do to help.

"I didn't expect to ever have a famous evangelist staying in our home. I don't know how to treat you!" she said.

"May I ask you a question?"

"Oh, yes," she said nervously.

"Who else are you expecting besides me?" I thought I had better find out so I could get nervous too.

"You're the one I'm talking about," she said.

I couldn't help but laugh. "Me? Where did you get the idea that I am famous?"

"From the 'Back to the Bible' magazine," she replied. "I'll show you." She soon returned with the magazine.

"Isn't that you?" she said as she pointed to the page.

"I have to admit it is me, but please, I don't think I am famous. I'm just a sinner saved by grace and called to preach. But thank you for making my day." From that time on, we got along very well.

11

MONKEY MEAT

That week at camp was a new and different experience. It was intimidating to preach to people who knew as much about the Bible as I did. I learned, however, that people can know what the Bible says but not obey it.

One of the missionaries tried to assure me. "Just preach to us. Many have the idea that they have 'arrived' spiritually just because they know the Bible. They put themselves on a pedestal just because they are pastors or missionaries." I knew I had my work cut out for me.

The meetings were to go from Monday through Saturday morning. I was the main speaker. There were lots of activities for all ages, but the children and teenagers mostly played soccer. They invited me to play, but I told them I like my legs just the way were and didn't want them broken. I took some walks, but never strayed from the main trails, for there were ant hills five feet high off the trails. The missionaries told me these ants could strip all the leaves from a huge tree overnight. One activity I enjoyed was the siesta. I wish it would become popular in the United States.

The meals at camp were very good. I ate breakfast with the Shoafs. I sometimes ate lunch and supper with the Brazilians, but I was afraid that what they ate would not agree with me. I did notice that some of the pastors were not too friendly.

The Lord laid on my heart various messages for the morning and evening services. I preached, but nothing happened. Some of the missionaries began to pray while I was preparing messages. On Friday night things broke loose. After the message, I began to pray. I heard crying from the audience. When I finished praying I looked up to see men, women, young people and children on their knees confessing their sins, especially their sin of pride. I told the missionaries not to do a thing, but to just pray and let the Lord take control. God was doing something unusual and wonderful. Some people spent the night on their knees. They were not going to be the same again, for God was going to use them. I went back to my room to rest.

The next day I perceived that the missionaries were unhappy about something. "What's wrong?" I asked them, but no one would tell me anything. Finally a missionary told me that the pastors wanted to show me their gratitude for preaching to them by having a special dinner for me.

"What is wrong with that?" I wanted to know.

"You'll find out soon enough," he growled, and walked away.

Now I was puzzled. Every time a pastor met me he smiled and tried to talk to me, or he shook my hand or hugged me. I had no idea what they were trying to say to me. All the Brazilian pastors seemed excited about the upcoming meal, but not the missionaries.

The time came for the banquet. One of the missionaries remarked, "Well, it's time for our last meal before we go home." The way he said it made me think it was going to be my last meal, period! They brought out plates of food loaded with salad, vegetables, rice and a piece of round meat. "What is that meat?" I whispered to the missionary sitting next to me.

"I'm not going to tell you. They just asked you to pray," he informed me.

I prayed, but I'm afraid I was a hypocrite. Instead of being thankful for the food, I was secretly hoping that meat would disappear. It didn't.

"Is it monkey meat?" I asked the missionary.

"I said I'm not going to tell you. And since you are the guest of honor, they are waiting for you to take the first bite." He didn't encourage me the way he said it.

I managed to take that first little bite of meat. The pastors smiled and happily dove right in. The missionaries, though, ate slowly with little mirth. I managed to stomach a little so I wouldn't offend the native pastors.

After it was all over, we went to pack up. I was going back to the Phillips's house in São Paulo. While putting my luggage in the trunk of a car, I said to one of the missionaries who didn't know me well, "That monkey meat wasn't too bad, was it?"

"Oh, how did you find out what it was?" He seemed surprised that I knew.

"I just guessed, and now you have confirmed my suspicions."

"Well," he said, "just be glad you weren't in the jungle. If the chief of a tribe likes you, he'll give you the head of the monkey along with the eyes and brains."

"I would make sure he hated me," I replied.

"If you did that," he warned me, "you wouldn't live to tell about it."

No way was I going to go down the Amazon River to visit various tribes! I have enough afflictions without adding to them. Now if people see me scratching my head or stomach or eating bananas, I tell them it is because I ate monkey meat.

Soon I was boarding my flight from São Paulo to Fortaleza. I landed at a small open-air airport. The Johnsons were there with their two daughters to meet me. It was a very hot area, so I didn't mind the cold showers.

Fortaleza was beautiful city. Located there was the Fortaleza Christian Academy for the missionaries' children, operated under the direction of Rev. and Mrs. Charles Johnson. I had the privilege of speaking at the academy and at churches in the area. I got really upset when Rev. Johnson took me to the Catholic church. Handicapped people were there begging for money.

"Why aren't they asking for food?" I asked.

"Just watch and you'll see," Rev. Johnson replied.

Soon the priest came out of the church and took the money the handicapped had collected and in return gave them some bread and rice to eat.

"Why does the priest take their money?"

"The priests just use the handicapped to get money to build their beautiful churches," Rev. Johnson told me. "The poor and afflicted mean nothing to the priest."

I enjoyed my time in Brazil with the missionaries and people who loved the Lord. All too soon it was time for me to return home. I missed my family too, and I could hardly wait to get home to report how God had used me, a man who wasn't supposed to be capable of doing all of this.

I flew to Bélem about nine p.m. and arrived about eleven p.m. I had a five-hour layover before catching my flight on to Miami. The airport was small and open-aired like the one in Fortaleza, but had small stores all around it. The devil began using my imagination to work on me again. I was sure that someone was going to mug me in this place and steal my belongings.

I finally asked the Lord to help me change my thinking. I began to meditate on various verses and promises from the Bible. About this time a young Brazilian man in a uniform walked over to me and said something in Portuguese. I said I didn't understand what he was saying.

He smiled broadly and said in English, "That's all right. I am a security guard here, but it is so quiet in the middle of the night that I get bored. I hoped you were an American so I could speak with you and practice my English. I learned it from a missionary here in Bélem."

When I told him I was a missionary and evangelist, his face lit up. He began to tell me about Stan Best and other missionaries in the area. After a long conversation, I asked him about his own spiritual condition. He said he was saved, but he admitted he was not really living for the Lord. We had a long talk about his life and what the Lord may have for him in the future. Before I boarded my flight, we had prayer together for the Lord's direction in his life. He thanked me, and I thanked the Lord for taking away my own fears to that I might be a servant to others. I didn't expect to ever see this young man again until I got to glory.

Several years passed. I became acquainted with Stan Best, and he invited me to preach in Bélem. After I preached a man ran over and hugged me. Was I ever surprised! It was that same man to whom I had talked for several hours at the airport. I was reminded of the fact that we never know why the Lord puts us in certain places at certain times, but we need to be faithful to serve Him wherever we are.

Once when I was with the Johnson family in Barbalha,

Brazil, I was asked to help start a school for the afflicted. The mayor's wife was a Christian and was very interested in having a school for these people. She persuaded her husband to call a town meeting. They met with the other city officials and the parents of the handicapped children. We had a long discussion about what type of school they needed and where it should be built. They decided to build it outside the city limits and use half the building for mentally retarded children and the other half for the physically handicapped. The teachers would have to learn by doing, and the parents said they would help out. The mayor's wife also thought the school should have devotions every day to try to reach the families for Christ. The school began and is still in operation today.

A SICKNESS UNTO DEATH

Some years later when I was in Brazil, I rode a bus to Barbalha. After riding all night, I arrived early in the morning at the bus station. The Johnsons were again there to greet me.

When we arrived at the Johnsons' home, there were people standing around with tears running down their faces. Brother Johnson explained that a loved one had passed away, and the funeral was to be that afternoon.

"Would you like to visit the family's home where the dead man is laid out, and go to the funeral?" he asked me. "It is something that you never see back in the States."

"Yes, I would like to go." On the way he told me about the coffin used by poor families. It had a false bottom that allowed the body to fall into the grave for burial. Then they took it back home to be used for the next one who died. He said that was once done in the early days of the United States too.

When we arrived at the house, a lady was wiping the dead man's face with cool water while others fanned the body. "The dead have to be buried within twenty-four hours in this climate," Rev. Johnson said. "There isn't any embalming down here."

After a short time of prayer, we walked to the cemetery with the men carrying the coffin. The dead man was a Christian and apparently had had a radiant Christian testimony. He had died shortly after being stricken with a liver ailment. A couple of days later another man died of this same liver disease, which had no cure.

A few days later I noticed I looked heavier, and I had a pain in my side. Brother Johnson took me to see a Dr. Williams. He examined me, and told us I had this incurable liver ailment that had killed the two Brazilian men. He wanted to hospitalize me immediately for an operation. I told him to forget it, for if this liver ailment was incurable an operation wasn't going to help.

I returned to my room, which had an air conditioner. I stayed in bed and drank as much water as I could. I continued to preach every day, either sitting up or reclining with my head propped, and people continued to get saved.

One day Doris Johnson came into my room to have a heart-to-heart talk. Her tone was very serious as she asked, "Bill, what do you want us to do with your body after you die?"

"Well, why don't you ship me back home in a box since I already have a return airline ticket," I joked.

"This is no time to be funny," she said. "Should I call your wife and let her know you may not be coming home? If so, when should I call? And if not, how do you want us to handle all of this?"

I had to face the reality of death, something I had not thought much about since my heart attack many years before. I told Doris I would write letters to take care of things. The first was to Betty, telling her that I loved her and that I was sick, but I would be fine and would see her soon. I didn't want her to worry. The second letter was to our pastor, Steve Davison, telling him I was on my death bed. "Please do not tell Betty" I wrote to him, "but do PRAY!"

I languished on my bed while the illness took its course. After three weeks, I noticed I wasn't hurting as much as before, and my swollen body seemed to be shrinking a little. Before another week had passed, my body was back to normal and all my pain had disappeared. I was still weak, but I decided to try to return home. Brother Johnson accompanied me back to Fortaleza, where

I preached in a couple of churches. He arranged for Brother Stan Best to meet me at the airport in Bélem to assist me in getting on the plane to Miami. Brother Best talked to me about adding Bélem to my list of churches to preach in when I returned to Brazil. It was good to talk about the future again instead of my funeral arrangements. I finally arrived back in Miami and made the connection to fly on to Gainesville, for these large aircraft were unable to land at Ocala.

Betty was there to meet me at the airport. When she saw me, her faced revealed her concern. "What is wrong with you? You look so pale and weak."

"Let's sit down, and I'll tell you all about it. You almost lost your husband." I told her what had taken place concerning my illness. I told her I had written to Pastor Davison and asked him not to tell her how seriously ill I was.

"I wondered why Ann Wisdom wanted to pay for me to fly to Fortaleza," Betty said. " 'Don't you want to see Bill?' she kept asking. 'I understand he isn't feeling well. I'll pay for your round-trip ticket.' Bill, why didn't you tell me?"

"I didn't want you to know because I know that you would worry yourself sick," I told her. "And besides, I was sure the Lord wasn't finished with me yet."

I made an appointment to see our family doctor, Dr. Lilly, to find out what exactly was wrong with me. After taking a blood test, he said he was amazed that I was still walking around. My blood was full of all sorts of poisons. He gave me various pills to clear up all the disease toxins, and warned me to stay away from hospitals and other sick people until I had completely recovered. Soon I was feeling fine and praising the Lord for giving my strength back and providing opportunities to testify about His goodness during my illness. I wrote to the missionaries back in Brazil to give them the good news about what the Lord had done for me. They wrote to me asking me to return, for my work in Brazil was not yet done.

I went back in 1992, my seventh trip to Brazil, to be with missionary Marvin Fray and talk about starting a school for the afflicted in Sao Paulo. I stayed a month and preached in area churches as well.

PREACHING IN AFRICA

Not long after my first trip to Brazil, I was in a missions conference at Calvary Baptist Church in Bradenton, Florida, where I met Dallas and Kay Washer. They were missionaries in Togo, West Africa, with their son and daughter-in-law, Ron and Ann Washer. Their ministry was with the blind, and they had a school and home for the blind in Togo. During the week they heard about my Brazil trip, and they invited me to be with them in Togo. We tried to come up with a date, but all our plans fell through.

Four years later we were all back at the same church for the same reason—missions conference. Again the Washers asked me to be with them in Kpalime, Togo. This time we were able to schedule a time for me to visit them in February 1990.

Everything was set for my trip to Africa, and then I received some news that made me very sad. Rev. Dallas Washer had gone to be with the Lord. I assumed my trip would be canceled, but I received a letter from Ron Washer asking me to continue my plans to be with him and the other missionaries in Togo. They had everything ready for me to preach. I was really excited. Africa! I could hardly believe the Lord had given me such an opportunity.

I invited a friend, Mr. Bill Shepard, to come with me to Togo. He was a senior vice president of the Sun Bank in Ocala, Florida, and he was able to take two weeks off to go to Africa. Bill and his wife, Debbie, had been married less than a year. Debbie encouraged Bill to go, but she warned him that he better be home for their first anniversary! This would be Bill's first missionary trip, and he didn't know what to expect. I didn't tell him. He would just have to learn by experience. Debbie packed a lot of dry foods in his luggage in case the food was too different from what he was used to. I didn't tell her that most missionaries ate like the rest of us.

We flew from Gainesville, Florida, to Atlanta. From there we flew to Brussels, Belgium, and on to Lome, Togo, on the Sabena airline. It was early February and cold when we left, but when we walked off the plane in Togo it was more than one hundred degrees.

Ron and Ann Washer met us. "Welcome to Togo!" Ron said, and handed me a Coke. "You need to drink it because you have a two-hour drive to our place. You'll be thirsty again before we arrive. In fact, you should drink a gallon of water a day while you are here."

"A gallon?" I exclaimed. "I don't drink that much water in a week!"

"You will now," Ron promised, and he was right. "It is so hot during the day that no one does much in the afternoon except lie down. The heat really saps your strength. And it isn't much cooler in the evenings."

A Togolese from the airport helped us pack our things in the Washers' van. We assumed everything was loaded, and off we went. When we arrived at about 11 p.m., Kay came out to welcome us to Kpalime.

As we carried our luggage into Ron's house, I couldn't find my raincoat. I asked Ron if someone else had taken it in. He said no, but he would look in the van. In a few minutes he returned with the bad news that the fellow at the airport who helped us with our luggage must have helped himself to my raincoat. "If you do not ask for something," Ron explained, "they assume they can have it."

"If that's the case, from now on I'm going to ask for everything I can!" I told him.

It was almost midnight before I got to bed, but just as I retired for the night Kay let me know that I would have the privilege of speaking to the blind at 6 a.m. the next morning. Bill Shepard wanted me to wake him in the morning so he could be in the service.

After a very short night of fitful sleep, I was up at 5:30 a.m. to get ready to preach through an interpreter. I tried to wake up Bill, but he pleaded with me to let him sleep, which I did. I was so groggy that I have no recollection of what I preached, but

God blessed His Word, and a blind teen-age girl received Christ as her Savior. My first convert in Africa! Afterward, although she could not see me, she could recognize the sound of my steps, and when she heard me walking outside she would make her way over to me and give me a big hug of appreciation.

Besides speaking at the blind center, I also spoke at several Baptist churches and at the missionaries' Christian school. Several others also came to know Christ as their Savior.

When I visited the hospital, I was given a grand tour of the operation—literally. When we came to the surgery room, the doctors were operating on a male patient.

"This is Rev. Maher and Mr. Shepard from Florida," the nurse said as she introduced us from the door.

"Come on in," the doctors said as they went on with their operation.

"Oh, we're not clean enough," I objected.

"That's all right. You can come in anyway."

"Uh, no, we'd better not distract you from your work," I said.

"Well, the next time you come to Togo, you'll have to plan to watch us operate," they said. *I'll never get back here,* I thought.

Those doctors were truly amazing. Besides witnessing to the patients at the hospital, they hold services and start churches. I don't know how they found time to do all that they do for the Lord. Everyone I met was doing a wonderful work for the Lord, just like the missionaries in Brazil.

Bill Shepard left for home in the middle of the month, while I stayed on until the end of February. I had a wonderful time with all of the missionaries and the people of Togo. Soon it was my time to return home. I was taken to Lome to have a couple of meetings before I left. One of the missionaries took me to a French restaurant where I ordered fish with herbs. When the waiter asked what herbs I wanted with the fish, I said, "French fries." Although the waiter didn't speak English, he understood what I said, and he laughed. The meal was delicious.

My last day in Togo was very busy. I preached to the missionaries and in a Baptist church. I rushed back to a missionary's house to shower and change clothes for the trip home. I arrived at the airport and rushed through customs, then waited for the call to board the plane back to Brussels. When the boarding call came, I had to point out my luggage before I boarded so it could be checked for bombs. Finally I was on the plane and excited to be heading back home.

I was very tired when I reached my seat, but happy because of what God had done. I was rejoicing in the Lord. It was after midnight when the plane took off, but the lady sitting next to me was nervous and began to talk to me in French. I wanted to get some sleep! I tried to be polite, but I would nod off to dreamland despite her chatter. When I did she would nudge me in the ribs.

Finally I called the flight attendant to tell the woman to speak English because I could not understand French. He told her, but she did not speak English. That didn't stop her incessant talking, though. I guess she figured that if she couldn't sleep, I couldn't either.

By the time I reached Brussels I was worn out. One of the flight attendants had pity on me. She took my briefcase and led me to a small room in the airport so I could rest before my flight left for Atlanta. Now, however, it was about seven-thirty a.m., and other people were also resting in the room. One of them asked me if I was from the United States. I told him I was, which was the wrong thing to say, for he and others decided they wanted to practice their English on me. I was in no mood to be an English teacher, but I tried to be gracious and talked to them. I had now been awake twenty-four hours straight.

At last, at about two p.m., the stewardess came to see how I was doing and learned that I still hadn't gotten any rest. She told me to follow her once more. After talking to the person in charge of boarding, she led me onto the empty plane so I could get some rest before the other passengers boarded. Just about the time I got to sleep, the other passengers started to board. People were talking excitedly and tossing luggage and bags in the storage compartments. No sleep for me all the way home to Atlanta.

When we landed, I had a hard time getting out of my seat. I hadn't slept in forty-two hours. A flight attendant helped me walk off the plane, and another helped me through customs. I thanked her for all the help they had given me. Someone else had gotten my luggage for me, and a young fellow was waiting for me with a wheelchair. He pushed me all the way to the gate where my plane was to leave for Gainesville.

We landed at Gainesville and someone again helped me off and down the ramp. Another wheelchair was waiting for me, but I told them I would walk so my wife would not be too worried about me. There was Betty with Bill and Debbie Shepard. I could tell she was concerned by the expression on her face. They were all worried about me, but I told them I was fine, except that I hadn't slept in forty-four hours.

After picking up my luggage, we drove forty-five minutes to our house. We talked all the way. I couldn't wait to hit the bed, but Betty had other ideas. She wanted to hear all about the trip.

"Wait a minute!" I protested. "Don't you realize I haven't slept in forty-six hours?"

She didn't pay any attention to me. She just put on some coffee and made some toast. We talked some, and then I realized what my wise wife was trying to do. She was helping me to relax so I could rest well. After a nice American shower, I was finally relaxed and ready to sleep after fifty-one hours of wakefulness.

I awoke and noticed the room was bright with daylight. I assumed I had slept for twenty-four hours. I got up and went to find Betty.

"What are you doing up?" she inquired.

"Why do you ask?" I answered. "I must have slept for a full day."

"You have not, Bill. You have slept only eight hours. You just arrived this morning."

"Let me see what time it is in Togo," I told her. "It is eight-thirty p.m. Togo time. I can seen I am going to have trouble getting back to Eastern time."

In 1994 I returned to Togo with Keith and Karon Baumann and Bill Shepard.

I have taken other foreign preaching trips over the years. When the Dooleys visited our church, they asked me to be with them in Chile after they returned. Later, Mark Henzler spoke at our missions conference and also asked me to come to Chile.

BACK TO SOUTH AMERICA

On May 29, 1992, Bill Shepard and I headed for Chile. Bill would return on June 6 while I went on to Brazil on June 13 to where I hoped to stay until July 22. We left from Orlando on an all-night flight to Santiago, Chile. We arrived in beautiful, cool weather. Bill Dooley was there to meet us, and he took us to his house where we met his family and rested up from our trip. It was our privilege to meet many missionaries and Chilean pastors in the time we were there. Bill Dooley and Mark Henzler acted as my interpreters, and souls were saved. They even arranged for me to have special meetings at their Bible institute, where I preached twice a night. The auditorium was filled each night, with the crowd overflowing all the way out to the street. God blessed the preaching of His Word with some wonderful results.

On March 23, 1993, I had the opportunity to return to Chile. Again we were blessed with wonderful results. This time the missionaries arranged some special meetings for me in a city called Rancagua. We held two services a night in the city auditorium, which the city officials allowed us to use for free. It was the first time that something like this had taken place in the city, and many souls were saved, and many who were away from the Lord returned to Him. I again spoke at the Bible institute, and I especially enjoyed speaking at the pastors' fellowship meetings. On April 15, I returned home rejoicing in the Lord.

In 1995 I went to Brazil for the seventh time. Missionaries Albert and Doris Johnson asked me to return to Fortaleza for two weeks of meetings. Keith and Karon Baumann, who accompanied me to Togo in 1994, were again with me.

We left Gainesville Airport and caught the Varig Airline from Miami to Fortaleza. The plane left on time but arrived at the Fortaleza airport three hours late. Brother Johnson was waiting for us. He took us to Fortaleza Academy for three hours' sleep, but we were too excited to sleep. We had only three hours because we had to make a rough, ten-hour bus ride to Barbalha. The bus was a good one, but the roads were terrible. The loud music on the bus made it impossible to sleep anyway. We enjoyed the ride despite the conditions. There was much to see and talk to Brother Johnson about. The last time I had been in Barbalha I had almost died.

We reached our destination about 11 p.m. Doris was waiting for us. After introducing the Baumanns to her, we headed for the Johnsons' nice home. Doris let me use their bathroom, where hot water was available. The Baumanns used the other one which had cold water only. "Oh, it can't be that cold!" they said. They soon changed their minds.

While I was there, the Johnsons prepared a surprise for me. Years before I had helped them start a school for the afflicted, and they wanted me to visit the children and their parents. I had the privilege to speak to them and take pictures.

"Hurry up," Brother Johnson said. "We have another place to visit."

"What place?" I asked.

"You'll see," said Brother Johnson with a smile.

We drove for an hour before we stopped in front of a beautiful building. When I stepped out, a lady shook my hand and led me into the building, laughing all the way. Inside were more people waiting for us—people with afflicted children. I was amazed at what I was seeing, but no one was saying anything. Brother Johnson was smiling too. "Please, tell me what this is all about," I begged him, but he wouldn't give me any information about what was going on.

We were led over to a table with cold water and coffee. "Why are they all sitting around looking at us and smiling?" I asked.

"Just wait and you will find out what has happened because of your ministry in our Brazilian state," Brother Johnson replied.

Finally a woman stood up and looked at me with a big smile. "We are so grateful you came to be with us today," she said. "We have always wanted to meet the person who started the school for the afflicted in Barbalha. If it hadn't been for you, we would not have this school." I could feel the tears in my eyes. "We came so we could thank you for caring for us as well as your own people," she went on. "Now we would like to hear from you and ask you some questions."

I don't remember what all I said, but I tried to communicate to them that it was my privilege to be used by the Lord to start various schools for the handicapped in their country and mine. Again, pictures were taken with the handicapped children and their parents. These children wanted to show me what they had accomplished as a result of hearing me say, " 'I can't' is not in the handicapped person's dictionary!" I left there rejoicing and amazed at what had been accomplished for the Lord with the afflicted.

We returned to Fortaleza, and an opportunity arose for me to speak at a bank. I was supposed to speak for forty-five minutes and then let them ask questions. An hour went by, but the people didn't leave for lunch and we continued. Finally Brother Johnson said to the people, "We will try and have Dr. Maher return in the future, and if he does we will have him return to the bank."

After speaking at the local Baptist church, we had to pack for our departure late at night. Several Brazilians came to the airport to see us off. Although it was a sad time, it was also a blessing, for many of them were saved under my ministry. It will be a joy to see them again if the Lord does indeed allow me to return to Brazil, or to see them in heaven if He does not.

DR. MAHER

Early in 1991 I was again at Mineral Heights Baptist Church in Greenville, Texas, having meetings. While I was there Betty called me to tell me to be sure to answer a letter she had sent on to me. She told me I should receive it the next day, but she didn't explain what the letter said or who it was from.

The next day the associate pastor came over the motel where I was staying to deliver this important letter. It was from Dr. Bob Jones, Jr. asking me if I would accept an honorary Doctor of Humanities degree from Bob Jones University. I would have to be on campus at their commencement exercises in order to receive it. The letter informed me that I had to let them know right away if I could come so they could reserve a room for my wife and me on campus. Furthermore, I was not to let anyone know about this.

I called over to the church and asked them if I could use a typewriter so I could reply to this urgent letter and mail it right away. Of course, everyone there was curious to know if I had a problem and why I had to hurry. They thought it must have been some kind of minor emergency.

From Greenville I went to be with Brother Bob Wallace at Galilean Baptist Church. When I arrived Brother Wallace said he received a phone call from my wife. "She said to tell you everything is all set. Does that make sense to you?" he asked.

"It makes more sense that you can imagine," I replied, and didn't tell him anything else although he tried to get some information out of me.

At last I arrived back home where Betty gave me all the details about our upcoming trip to Greenville, South Carolina. On May 3, 1991, we flew to Greenville, where a young man was waiting at the airport to take us to our room in the Campus View Apartments at the university. As soon as I arrived, people there who knew me asked why I was there. "It is graduation, isn't it?" I replied, and left it at that.

We were invited to eat with the Jones family, and with the staff and board members. Another old friend, Rev. Randy Carroll, was there. I just assumed he was there because he was a member of the board. Dr. Bob Jones, III told everyone to leave us alone and stop asking us questions, for we were his guests. From that time on we enjoyed ourselves without people asking, "Why are you here?"

We also were given tickets to the university's Shakespearean play. When we went to the play we discovered we were sitting with the dean of students, Mr. Jim Berg, and his family. They are members of Faith Baptist Church, and we had known them for years. They too knew we didn't usually attend the graduation activities, but they didn't ask why we were there. My wife had taught me to appreciate operas and plays, and I enjoyed the play very much.

The following morning after breakfast, those who were to receive degrees met at a designated room. To my surprise, there was Rev. Randy Carroll. We congratulated one another and then put on our caps and gowns and posed for pictures. Then we lined up outside for the long procession to Founder's Memorial Amphitorium where the degrees would be conferred.

We took our seats on the platform, and soon the ceremony began. I was among six who were getting honorary doctor's degrees. I kept scanning the audience, trying to spot Betty, but I couldn't find my short wife among the crowd. I did see my old friend, Dr. John Vaughn, pastor of Faith Baptist Church, who had received his honorary doctor's degree the year before. He had earned a master's degree, and his oldest daughter Debbie was to receive her bachelor's degree.

Soon it was time for me to march across the platform to receive my diploma. My old friend, Dr. Otis Holmes, read the citation as I stood smiling with tears streaming down my face. As I bent over to receive the blue and white cape, I heard Dr. Jones, Jr. say, "Dr. William T. Maher." That was me! The smile never left my face the whole commencement ceremony. Many of those who received earned degrees gave me a high sign or a handshake when they came to the platform. They were glad I was one of them, and I was glad to be one of them. I am proud to be a part of Bob Jones University. It has been a great privilege for me to teach and preach there several times over the years.

Afterward the Vaughns found me and mentioned their surprise at seeing me there. They took more pictures, and Pastor Vaughn invited me to speak at Faith Baptist Church on Sunday night. We again ate with the Joneses, board members, and those who had just received their honorary doctorates.

We were at the university church service the next day, which was Sunday. That night we were at Faith Baptist Church. I was glad they had a new church building so I wouldn't have to preach three times! After church they gave a small party for me and presented me with a new Bible from Hidden Treasure Christian

School. On Monday, May 6, we headed home. We were tired but happy, and grateful for the Lord's blessings.

When we arrived back home the phone rang. It was Brother Bob Wallace calling. "You rascal! When your wife called and said everything is all set, you knew what she meant and you never told me! Well, now I understand why you couldn't tell me. Congratulations!"

I then called the man who led me to Christ and got me started in the ministry, Rev. Geren, to give him the good news. He said he was proud of me, but he was still going to just call me "Bill."

"That's all right," I told him, "because you are still 'Ger' to me."

I have the "Reverend" and "Doctor" titles, but the ones I like best are "Uncle Bill," "Pop," or "Dad Maher," and now that I am a grandfather, "Papa" and "Grand Dad Maher." These titles aren't used by only my own relatives, but also by many of my spiritual children around the country and the world. There is even a Christian man in Santiago, Chile, who calls me Father Abraham Bill, for he says I have children in many nations.

WHO WOULD HAVE DREAMED IT?

An honorary doctorate, preaching all over the country and in foreign lands, broadcasting "The Courage and Hope Hour" for thirty-two years-all of this has happened to a fellow who was born afflicted, who the doctors said would never be able to do anything important. But God doesn't make any mistakes. According to Romans 8:28, "All things work together for good to them that love God, to them who are the called according to his purpose." Those doctors sure didn't know what our Lord and Savior Jesus Christ can do with a person who surrenders to Him.

Now I am sixty-eight years old, but I hope this isn't the end of the story. I have no idea what else will happen, but I don't believe in retirement. I want to continue to be used by God until He takes me home. I love staying busy for Him. Doing the Lord's work is the greatest thing that any human being can do. I do know my future is secure and safe in Him, either here or with

Him in heaven where I will one day receive a new and perfect body like His. Then I want to hear Him say to me those wonderful words found in Matthew 25:21, "Well done, thou good and faithful servant."

If you study the gospels, you will find that Jesus spent half or more of His time among the handicapped. How He must have loved them to spend so much time with them. In Luke 14:13, He pronounced a blessing on those who minister to the poor, the maimed, the lame, and the blind. I ask you, dear reader, how much time have you spent with the handicapped? What have you done to demonstrate to them the love of our Lord Jesus Christ? Do you realize that within every handicapped body there lives a soul for whom Christ died? Have you sought to bring them to Him? May God give you a burden, as he has given me, to reach the afflicted with the gospel of Jesus Christ.